SOUL TALK

SOUL TALK

THE NEW SPIRITUALITY OF AFRICAN AMERICAN WOMEN

AKASHA GLORIA HULL

Inner Traditions
Rochester, Vermont

Inner Traditions International
One Park Street
Rochester, Vermont 05767
www.InnerTraditions.com

Library of Congress Cataloging-in-Publication Data

Hull, Gloria T.
    Soul talk : the new spirituality of African American women /
Akasha Gloria Hull.
        p. cm.
    Includes bibliographical references.
    ISBN 0-89281-943-X (alk. paper)
    1. African American women—Religious life.

BL625.2 .H85 2001
291.4'082—dc21

                                                      2001016872

Printed and bound in the United States

10 9 8 7 6 5 4 3 2 1

Text design and layout by Rachel Goldenberg
This book was typeset in Apolline with Schneidler Initials as the display typeface

For Toni Cade Bambara

(March 25, 1939–December 9, 1995)

THESE BONES, THESE BONES
for TCB

Long black bones
waving like angry spears
under an ocean of years and water
clamoring fronds uprising
in the cold and tropical sea

Grandmother bones
Father bones
Baby bones thrown overboard
Those who leaped
who fell in the fight
They who saw the future
            and ran screaming into time
The rot which could not go
            unburied
The troubled spirits swept clean
            away by the avenging storm
Lovers who held each other's hand
            and went down singing

These African bones
that did not live
to tell their story
are troubling the waters
are asking the bone
            of their bone

their present flesh
the black bones
redbones
half-white bones
bleached bones
brown bones
their bones
colored forever
in the dyes of history
about the unpoured libations
the monuments which do not rise
not even in our imaginations
are wondering how we came
to this place of forgetfulness
with not even a pile of stones
to mark the sacred plot

Akasha (Gloria T.) Hull

Author's note: "TCB" stands for "Toni Cade Bambara" and for "Taking Care of Business." I recited this poem at the Middle Passage Monument Ceremony on July 3, 1999, in New York City, after which a gravestone was lowered to the floor of the Atlantic Ocean, 427 kilometers off New York harbor. Given the long-standing absence of such markers, our books, paintings, and other forms of artistic expression, and all our acts of creative living and struggle, have historically been the surviving monuments to our ancestral spirits who perished during the infamous Middle Passage.

CONTENTS

Acknowledgments

For their willing and wonderful participation in this work, I pour forth gratitude to: Toni Cade Bambara, Lucille Clifton, Masani Alexis DeVeaux, Michele Gibbs, Dolores Kendrick, Geraldine McIntosh, Sonia Sanchez, Namonyah Soipan, and Alice Walker.

For grant support that gave me opportunities I would otherwise not have had for research, reflection, and writing, I gratefully acknowledge: The American Association of University Women, 1991; University of California, Santa Cruz, Committee on Research Awards; Djerassi Resident Artists Program, 1994; The National Humanities Center, 1994–95.

For their love, faith, encouragement, advice, and generous reading of varying portions of this book as I labored to write it, thanks and praise to: Debra Lynne Busman, above all, and to Mrs. Jimmie Thompson, Martha T. Zingo, Adrian Prentice Hull, Yasmina Porter, Namonyah Soipan, Geraldine McIntosh, Toni Morrison, Bettina Aptheker, Kate Miller, Ann T. Jealous, Alissa Goldring, Marilyn McKenzie, Faith Queman, Mary Alice Hayden, Cassandra Paden, Francis V. O'Connor, Cheryl Williams, Celine-Marie Pascale, Caroline Pincus, Denise Stinson, Sandra Dijkstra, Gareth Esersky.

For their consummate care of my words and this work, deep appreciation to the professionals at Inner Traditions and especially to my editor, Elaine Sanborn.

INTRODUCTION

A new spirituality has arisen among African American women. On one woman, it looks like the suddenly acquired ability to channel messages from her dead mother and from ascended beings. For another, it is the impetus that drives her to begin approaching political activism by searching for the "essential seed of birth and continuance" inside herself and others. For yet another woman, it manifests as the power to access divine creativity and give it a very specific, but still universally resonant, face.

Soul Talk investigates this new spirituality that is taking shape among many progressive African American women at this turning of the twenty-first century. Arising around 1980, it brings together three interlocking dimensions: 1) the heightened political and social awareness of the civil rights and feminist movements, 2) a spiritual consciousness that melds black American traditions such as Christian prayer and ancestral reverence with New Age modalities such as crystal work and self-help metaphysics, and 3) enhanced creativity, especially as represented by the outburst of

1

literature by Toni Morrison, Toni Cade Bambara, Alice Walker, Lucille Clifton, Octavia Butler, Audre Lorde, Ntozake Shange, Paule Marshall, Sonia Sanchez, Gayle Jones, Tina McElroy Ansa, Phyllis Alesia Perry, Sandra Jackson Opoku, and others—literature that foregrounds supernatural material, viscerally impacting an unprecedented number of readers.

Let me further define this spirituality and my terms. Political consciousness is locating the self in the mundane scheme where realities such as race, gender, and economics are profoundly considered and injustices of power and privilege are resisted. This awareness or consciousness among black people has historically fueled both the literal and symbolic spitting-in-the-faces-of-oppression that characterizes our struggles for freedom and recognition. Spirituality, as I view it, involves conscious relationship with the realm of spirit, with the invisibly permeating, ultimately positive, divine, and evolutionary energies that give rise to and sustain all that exists. In the guise practiced by a growing group of contemporary black women, this spiritual expression builds on firm cultural foundations and traditional Christian religions, but also freely incorporates elements popularly called "New Age"—Tarot, chakra work, psychic enhancement, numerology, Eastern philosophies of cosmic connectedness, and others. And, finally, creativity is what results when the ideas, originality, and beauty we apprehend in the world of spirit are given concrete form through our art and inspired daily living, whether that be a poem, painting, or novel, an original solution to one of our children's problems, or a pot of smoked turkey wings and greens.

These, then, are the three dimensions—politics, spiritual consciousness, and creativity—comprising the new spirituality this book aims to explore. Working together, they function as a fluid and dynamic interpenetrating triangle, with each dimension impacting the others and all of them together generating tremendous power. Far too often, political considerations are kept separate from spiritual matters, and the role that spirituality plays in creativity is cloaked or undervalued. What I see in the new spirituality as practiced by many African American women is a beautiful and compelling model for bringing the three dimensions together. Once tapped, its power is transforming: One woman walks into a formal corporate meeting and "calls together" all of her spiritual energy to correct the white officers deviating from human relations guidelines; another maintains two altars in her home where she regenerates and stills herself each day by lighting a candle or saying affirmations or thanking the universe, all in preparation for the work in the world that she feels called to undertake.

Toni Cade Bambara—to whom *Soul Talk* is dedicated—referred to the array of spiritual technologies comprising the New Age as "everybody's ancient wisdom." In so doing, she recognized that the expressions of spirituality labeled "New Age" today are, in fact, very old systems for spiritual attunement that appear in slightly differing forms but with the same essential content in all root cultures. Toni herself took very seriously her identity as a Pan-Africanist woman with socialist sympathies and honored the fact that, as she put it, her soul was having an adventure in that particular body. From the deep political commitments fostered by this flesh-and-blood, skin-and-bone identity, she made herself "available"—again, her word—to the behest of spirit, and then, attuned to those transpersonal energies, devised stunningly creative ways to write fiction, make videos, dance, and live for the purpose of effecting social and planetary justice.

My understanding of this new spirituality has not always been so neat and clear. Around 1980 I was, of course, aware that something strong and exciting was beginning to happen. In large numbers, African American women were feeling their power and feeling good about themselves. Especially for those of us who could take advantage of fresh opportunities, our lives had definitely been improved by the doors that had opened as a result of the agitation for civil rights—agitation in which some of us had personally participated. Significant segments of the population of African American women had also been favorably touched by the revolutions in female consciousness fostered by the women's movement and, indeed, some of us had helped establish black feminist networks and activities. The times were propitious, the energy heady. Things we had never before dreamed of seemed possible. I and many of my black women friends found ourselves reading New Age, metaphysical, and self-help books; using stones and herbs and crystals for healing and protection; traveling to other, particularly black, countries; and making large geographic, personal, and professional shifts in our lives. My spiritual sense told me that the insights about human potential contained in texts like Viktoras Kulvinskas's *Survival into the Twenty-first Century: Planetary Healers Manual* and Marilyn Ferguson's *The Aquarian Conspiracy: Personal and Social Transformation in Our Time* were essentially valid and not to be ignored.

In addition, a spectacular outpouring of literary work by African American women strikingly paralleled these lifestyle and consciousness-inducing changes. Books by authors such as Toni Morrison, Toni Cade Bambara, Alice Walker, and Gayle Jones deployed spiritual themes and supernatural material with a bold and impressive hand. In these works, through language that itself shimmers with a powerful otherworldly quality, the ordinary yet extraordinary characters reach beyond physical oppression into realms of healing and light, and ghosts and flying become much more than metaphor or figments of imagination. This literary renaissance was officially recognized, so to speak, when Toni Morrison appeared on the cover of *Newsweek* magazine in 1981 for an article that glowingly discussed her novels as "black magic" and also hailed these other three writers as "startling young voices—all female, gifted, and black."

At the time, I was aware of these developments, but was not, in any way, aware enough to theorize about them. In an essay I wrote elucidating Bambara's remarkable 1980 novel, *The Salt Eaters,* I tried to explain the novel's dense metaphysics and myriad spiritual technologies, ranging from astrology and reincarnation to Sufi tales and quantum physics. I even stressed that the purpose of her work was to heal the split between politics and spirituality—but I did not yet grasp how this unification may have been beginning to happen in real time, in our reality.

Not until 1991 did I realize that what was occurring with regard to spirituality in the lives and literature of African American women might be a large enough movement to warrant a book. In the course of envisioning and writing this book over the next ten years, I gradually came to understand the significance of the personal, literary, and social changes I had both participated in and observed—changes that have continued to unfold. Here, in a nutshell, is what I see.

I believe that humanity in general is in the midst of making a difficult transition into a period when accessing the spiritual dimensions of ourselves will enable us to function more optimally, and, ultimately, to create a better world. This is the transit from the Piscean to the Aquarian age spoken about in New Age writings. I recognize that black women's literature and life activities contribute in highly visible and important ways to this planetary movement. By pointing this out, I am deliberately adding race to the perceived New Age, and a black female perspective to Aquarian consciousness, revealing from this particular vantage point just how widespread and varied this current revolution in spiritual evolution really is. African American women's contributions remind us that consciousness about race and gender should exist among New Age thinking and agendas. In many quarters, the apolitical nature of much New Age activity gives the New Age a bad reputation. Opening up to the contributions and voices of black women may help to change that largely white, largely apolitical image. It goes without saying, too, that then the picture will be truer, more accurate, and more complete.

Reflecting on the rise of this new spirituality among African American women, I realize, further, that it helps to explain what appeared to be a slackening of political energy and activity around 1980. At the time, some dismayed politicos and various cultural observers were declaring that social activism was dead. After the bold strides of the civil rights and black power movements, and after the teeming ferment of the women's and feminist movement, it looked like nothing much was happening. In retrospect, this assessment is glaringly untrue. Transformative energy had not vanished, but was only quietly gathering itself before expanding to encompass an enlarged spirituality in order to effect even more positive changes, in order to "do" politics at a higher, more spiritualized frequency. It would not be inaccurate, even, to call this spiritual rise a "third revolution"—one that continues today. And perhaps it is not surprising that it began to occur during one of the most politically regressive periods of our country's history, when Ronald Reagan's tenure as the fortieth president of the United States brought straitened circumstances, hardships, and crises to many individuals and many progressive causes.

Today we can continue to add understanding to understanding, and pile insight on top of insight. Just as Toni Cade Bambara came to accept that writing—and particularly her writing—was, to quote her, "a legitimate way to participate in struggle," it may be appropriate at this point to similarly accept that *being spiritual* is also a legitimate way to participate in social struggle. If being spiritual means meditating to make connection with the larger self that is part and parcel of the greatest whole, and trying to see, feel, and know our oneness with it; if being spiritual means going to therapy in order to feel and heal our own pain so that we can identify with and heal the pain of others; if it means traveling to Machu Picchu or Egypt to enlarge our vision of the world beyond our own backyards, money worries, and personal problems; if being spiritual means taking up Tibetan Buddhism to open our hearts and minds so that we are moved to alleviate suffering and misery wherever we encounter it, in whatever way we can; if it means seeking transcendent merging with the whole so that we no longer name as "other" those who are different from us and those whose life scripts challenge us to get outside our own comfort zones; if it means doing yoga to reduce the stress and tension ballooning inside us so that we can open our eyes to the world around us and really be present in it; if it means visualizing our health and prosperity as pieces of the health and prosperity of every living being; if being spiritual means all of these kinds of things, then, surely, it is a more-than-legitimate way to participate in struggle. Unfortunately, the service aspect of spirituality is glaringly absent from too many spiritual books and activities.

Nurturing such a broadly conceived spirituality, we would, I believe, find ourselves acting politically—that is, spontaneously intervening in situations where detrimental inequities of power and privilege are operating, and doing so in ever more creative and effective ways. By so doing, we move from politics to spirituality to creativity, and back again to politics, with not only our flesh-and-blood identities but also our breath-and-spirit soul selves engaged. Thus armed, so to speak, we are ready for the "wide, long battle" that Sonia Sanchez predicts will be waged "on a very spiritual level" to try to get people to move.

The union of politics, spirituality, and creativity holds tremendous potential for both personal and collective transformation. As practiced by contemporary black women, this three-dimensional spirituality begins to reveal the future visions that can redeem our world. One such vision came to Lucille Clifton through messages that she channeled from a group of ascended teachers who called themselves The Ones Who Talk (see chapter 7), messages that she turned into short, pithy poems. While The Ones Who Talk transmitted the same old lessons, "the same old / almanac: january / love one another / february / whatever you sow / you will reap," they also gave a more stringent warning to "balance / or be balanced" before the universe, grown impatient, might "slowly / turn its back" and "walk away." In this critical New Age, what many African American women model is a spirituality that can help us all to learn in good time how to love our collective self and vivify the planet so that we can be part of the universe, and it, in turn, can inhabit us.

Having realized in 1991 that a story needed to be told about this new black women's spirituality, I set out to do so. Although I had what Toni Cade Bambara would call a "mandate," that was all I had. My initial efforts were tentative and groping. I soon figured out, however, that interviewing other African American women should be the first step. Eventually, I spoke extensively with nine interesting and powerful women. Five of them have national and international reputations as writers: Lucille Clifton, Dolores Kendrick, Sonia Sanchez, Toni Cade Bambara, and Alice Walker. Upon reflection, it made perfect sense to me that the guiding intelligence inherent in spiritual energy would use writers as appropriate vehicles for touching masses of people. The other four women are likewise positioned in influential roles. They are revolutionary artist Michele Gibbs; professor-writer Masani Alexis DeVeaux; corporate human resources specialist Geraldine McIntosh; and holistic psychotherapist Namonyah Soipan. I chose these women because I felt that I knew them well, and because I believed we could speak together candidly, freely, spontaneously, and intimately. The basic questions I put before each one were: *How do you see yourself as a spiritual being, and how does that spirituality manifest itself in your life and work?*

I decided to talk first with **Lucille Clifton.** I wanted her to speak about herself as a "two-headed" woman. Throughout diasporic African cultures, people such as healers, savants, and rootworkers who possess innate, intuitive insight into the invisible world are termed *two-headed,* which signifies that they have a command of that world as well as the everyday, external one that is considered by most people to be real. Lucille is, foremost, a mother of six grown children (one now deceased); a native of the poor, hardworking steel mill and ghetto communities of Buffalo, New York, and Baltimore, Maryland; a fine and prolific poet highly respected by her peers; a writer of beautifully affirming children's books; and a university professor.

Struck by the complex simplicity of her poems and their glistening immersion in otherworldly truths, and fortified by the acquaintance I had deepened with her as we both taught literature at the University of California, Santa Cruz, I enlisted her as my very first interview subject. Lucille was more than wonderful—frank and open, funny, generous—and she validated completely what I had sensed about the richness of spiritual vision in her work. Without obfuscation or preciousness, she talked to me about her unsought, unexpected contact with her deceased mother sixteen years after her death, and the impact that this had made on her, her family, her work, and her spiritual growth. Lucille's clean, fine consciousness about a world we normally do not openly acknowledge affirmed the direction I had chosen and encouraged me to go on.

After Lucille, I conversed over the next three years with the other eight women, in the order in which I speak about them here.

During her long career, **Dolores Kendrick** helped to design the university without walls program in Washington, D.C., and taught for a number of years at Philips Exeter Academy in New Hampshire.

When I heard Dolores read from her newly published 1989

book of poems written in the voices of African American slave women, I recognized their authentic fire and responded very deeply to them. Hers is the type of poetry that, in Emily Dickinson's words, blows off the top of my head and has always called to me. Discovering Dolores's poems made me want to know more about her and her work. I was also struck by the fact that they presented insistent voices of slavery that were increasingly and tumultuously making themselves heard. Coming from her background as a deeply faithful and practicing Catholic, Dolores speculated with grounded clarity about why these buried stories sought new life through her. Our conversations, which were the only ones conducted by telephone, could not have been more probing or satisfying had they been carried on face-to-face.

Michele Gibbs is a published writer and poet, a seasoned organizer, now a visual artist and sculptor, and an American Studies Ph.D. from Brown University. I met Michele in the late 1970s when we both were trying very hard to change the system of education to include more and more relevant material about black people and women, and black women in particular. In and out of each other's orbits for years, we made especially close alignment when I lived in Jamaica in the mid-1980s with my husband and son. Michele visited us there while she helped to paint a mural in Falmouth and recharted her life course. Her radical critique of U.S. politics and culture, and her independent life that was a living revolution is what attracted me to her. As the child of an interracial black-and-white communist couple, Michele fashioned her own organic and holistic spirituality from the inquiring and skeptical mind her parents fostered in her. It has led her to Oaxaca, Mexico, where she lives in rhythmic harmony with indigenous North American people and the natural world.

Masani Alexis DeVeaux's poetry, short stories, and plays have been published, have been performed on stage, and have appeared on television. Having more than proved her mettle as a "young writer," she has expanded into the ranks of critic and university professor, completing her Ph.D. in English in 1997 at the State University of New York, Buffalo.

Masani and I met through the burgeoning friendships and creative circles of the black feminist 1980s. We were drawn together by vital cultural sharing such as the original and witty dramatic performances she and Gwendolen Hardwick produced in New York City. Passionate about black women's lives and literature, she is particularly exuberant regarding the role we play in enlarging human consciousness. Drawn from an array of traditions, her self-defined spirituality hinges on "doing something" in acknowledgment of the divine each day.

Geraldine (Geri) McIntosh currently earns her living as a diversity consultant based in Wilmington, Delaware. She is a remarkable woman—street-smart, on her own since she was seventeen, good with money and numbers, wise in the ways of the world, possessing what she terms "people" skills.

For a while in the mid-1970s, Geraldine and I partnered with each other, but the true tone of our relationship is sibling, with me as the slightly older and more conventional sister. From within the depths of her own spiritual being and her rich experiential life, Geraldine has arrived at complex insights about connection, love, and constant growth as the essence of spirituality. Her mission seems to be to use all that she is and all that she possesses toward infusing heart and soul into the workings of corporate America for the immediate benefit of women and people of color.

Having turned me toward a healthy diet and dreadlocks in

1979, a black woman friend named Konda introduced me to **Namonyah Soipan** a year or so later. Namonyah is a world-traveler (who underwent initiation with the Masai in Kenya); a self-created sartorial work of art; a Ph.D. candidate in transpersonal psychology and African mysticism; and a holistic psychotherapist who works with African and Native American shamanic medicine. In addition to the United States, she has trained in Japan, Amsterdam, and throughout the United Kingdom. She is currently formulating workshops, rituals, and a book called "Activating Your Thunder" on healing women from sexual abuse. After living and working in London, England, she has returned to the United States and is reestablishing her practice in California.

As time passed, our mutual respect and friendship grew and, despite living oceans apart, we kept up with each other. Together in Ghana, we had a fantastic interchange about comparative spirituality, her practice of ancestor reverence, and the whys and wherefores of living a spiritual life. Our Baptist church backgrounds meshed, as did our constant seeking of spiritual homes along many different paths.

Sonia Sanchez is a longtime resident of New York City and Philadelphia, the mother of grown twin sons, and a professor of English at Temple University. As a leading figure—and a strong female one—of the New Black Poetry movement of the 1960s and 1970s, she wrote with a voice that immediately struck my ear. Her many volumes of poetry have been highly praised and prize-winning. I have continued ever since to follow her career and promote her work, which is unparalleled in its craft and fervor. Always warm and committed to righteous change, she more than once has thanked sister critics such as myself for the symbiotically nurturing relationship we forge with her and other black women writers. If spirituality does not serve the cause of socio-racial liberation, Sonia has no use for it. In her work, her aim is to transform every stage from which she speaks into an altar and a shrine.

Sitting at a lunch table in Alabama sometime in the mid-1980s with Bernice Johnson Reagon, Barbara Smith, Patricia Bell Scott and **Toni Cade Bambara,** as we consulted together on a curriculum transformation project, I asked Toni if she would be my spiritual teacher. She almost laughed me under the table, she who—she said—could barely keep her own life together, let alone have somebody else following her around. Despite this refusal, everything Toni has written, every word she has spoken, every contact I had with her, has been an indelible lesson on how to yoke spirituality, politics, art, and everyday life. Toni's two books of short stories and her novel, *The Salt Eaters,* give some of those lessons to the world, while she herself lived them out in her career as dancer, author, community organizer, lecturer, videographer, and mother. Toni's spirituality attracted me because it is metaphysics that is highly intellectual and occult, as well as revolutionary and black. I have been able to sit at her proverbial feet now that she has passed on even more than when she was alive, and her central place in my seeking consciousness is why I offer *Soul Talk* to her.

I met **Alice Walker** around 1974–75 when those of us interested in women's studies invited her to the University of Delaware and she read from *In Love and Trouble: Stories of Black Women* (1973). As a member of the Feminist Press Reprints Advisory Committee, I helped to facilitate her 1979 collection of Zora Neale Hurston's work. Over the years, we corresponded sporadically and have had a few contacts and visits. I love Alice for her writing and politics, and for being herself. In this final respect, she is a model of self-confidence and uniqueness toward which we all can aspire. Her numerous writings—poetry, short fiction, novels, essays, and memoir—have brought her worldwide fame, particularly her stellar novel, *The Color Purple* (1982). Alice embraces a religion of love for all of God's marvelous creations, and fights tirelessly for the right of them all to "bloom."

The conversations I had with each of these women were unique. Always, I led with some version of my question, "How do you see yourself as a spiritual being, and how does that spirituality manifest itself in your life and work?" Then, I went with the flow. Because I did not precisely see what the project I was working on would become, I had no defined areas that I asked every woman to address, no list of pre-formulated questions. Moreover, at the time of the interviews I was just approaching the path of my own genuine spirituality. I was very opinionated, too much in love with my own limited ideas and points of view, and in a way, too full of myself.

But these same qualities also rendered me inquisitive, persistent, and single-minded when I was going after something. This led me to ask the right questions, elicited just the right information (both basic and unusual), and precipitated some of the most fruitful arguments and exchanges—for example, with Masani Alexis DeVeaux about what kinds of actions constituted being spiritual, or with Namonyah Soipan about her need to carry around her *eguns* (ancestors) in a "pot," or with Dolores Kendrick about the possible superiority of "channeled" writing. The interactions between me and all these women were blessed and special. Some force beyond ourselves took us to places we never dreamed we would go, on occasion startling the women into exclamations such as, "I can't believe I'm saying this," or "Something is going on here." I believe it was all about the energy that wanted, finally, to become this book. I feel boundless gratitude toward these wonderful women for participating in this work.

Imagine ten audio tracks of women, all speaking at once their truths, with sometimes open, sometimes unexpressed vitality and passion. This outpouring bubbled with life, but was also chaotic, overwhelming, and a little confusing. *Soul Talk* has ultimately taken its final shape because of four guiding factors. First of all, I consciously decided to incorporate myself and my experiences freely, to really *be* one of the "African American women" I was talking and theorizing about, rather than distancing myself as some kind of detached observer. This gave me an entire additional "data set" to work with, so to speak, and was enormously helpful in fleshing out the points I wished to make. Including my life was even more essential in the writing of chapter 5, where I tackle the difficult subject of the sexual abuse of children.

Secondly, after I pored repeatedly over the interview transcripts, I saw—rather painfully—that all this material was not going to organize itself easily and gracefully and that I would simply have to impose an order on it, based on the topics that I could glean from what was there. Hence, these seven chapters that, in the end, are a very valid reflection of what the nine women talked about—their religious history, their concept of and brushes with spirit, their growing up years and life trajectories, their work and artistic and creative process, their sense of themselves as African American women in a racist, sexist, classist, and heterosexist society, and their ideas about the state of the world. Proceeding through the book from chapter 1 through chapter 6, the reader engages the wealth of experience that impacts upon and determines this new spirituality until, by chapter 7, politics, spirituality, and creativity have come together at a higher turn of the spiral.

Thirdly, connected to this organizational scheme was my decision not to produce what essentially would have been a book of interviews. Instead of simply presenting the material as it came, I used what was said as provocative seedlings and sprouting nodes, establishing conceptual frameworks, explaining, exploring, embellishing according to my perceptions of both the mundane and the spiritual world. For instance, when Geraldine McIntosh raps about the universal spirit to which she feels connected and which connects her to everyone else, I step in with commentary about the qualities of the soul. Or when Alice Walker assiduously resists viewing herself as a medium for her novel *The Color Purple*, I use her resistance as the opportunity to lay out what I apprehend about the mechanism and magic of spiritual creation. And, of course, everything that I say in chapter 6 about figures as diverse as Oprah Winfrey and Hillary Rodham Clinton participating in the twenty-first century movement of women conducting spiritual power is my own reading. The general stature of these two women is verified by the fact that, in a December 2000 Gallup poll, Clinton topped the list of women most admired by Americans, with Winfrey (tied with Margaret Thatcher) garnering second place. Taking them up as subjects for serious and respectful discussion is one of the strategies I employ to try to bridge the gap that exists between the attitudes and points of view of those who consider themselves critical intellectuals and those who are considered by these intellectuals to be less independently thoughtful.

Lastly, what *Soul Talk* has ultimately become has everything to do with the final piece of inspiration that shaped it—that is, my finally seeing that what makes this new spirituality of African American women truly remarkable is its three-pronged nature: its pronounced political and social awareness, eclectic spiritual consciousness, and creativity. I spent a long time working out in my head and diagramming on paper what politics, spirituality, and creativity were and graphing both the independent and symbiotic interrelationships they could have with each other. Once I saw that this triangle of energies defined the spirituality I was trying to grasp, I felt that I had something solid, significant, and original to offer. Someone else looking at the same social configurations and interview material could see something different. However, this particular formula spelled "Eureka" for me.

What I am saying about the current manifestation of spirituality being comprised of these three interpenetrating dimensions does not mean that black women, or indeed women, or indeed both men and women in other seasons and epochs have not displayed these same linked qualities of political consciousness, spiritual awareness, and sharp creativity. Among African American women, we can call to mind heroic figures like Harriet Tubman, or Zora Neale Hurston, or Fannie Lou Hamer and see these attributes on display. However, the degree and extent of this contemporary movement is unprecedented—*all* this recent identity-heightening political activism, *all* these remarkable books pouring out at the same time, and *all* this talk, everywhere we turn, about spirituality. It goes beyond individual attainment into the realm of a group phenomenon. It is an in-our-faces happening that is both culturally specific and in tandem with the changing times. Seeing this gave *Soul Talk* its overarching message.

So, from the point of bubbling possibility contained in what I earlier spoke of, metaphorically, as interview sound tracks, I took those tracks, lined them up, and was able—after much listening and a good deal of fiddling with the controls—to hear the seven cuts of creative music that they made. After that, it was a matter of dubbing out the inessentials and harmonizing what remained, and then giving the production an overall theme. Because of the life that is in it and the spirit that birthed it, I trust that the composition plays. My role was to have the vision and the drive, to seek out the necessary material, and then—using the entirety of my internal and external resources—put it in a form that made sense and could be shared. This final form blends biography, autobiography, interviews, literary critique, film analysis, spiritual teaching, and cultural commentary into a whole that, like the spirituality that spawned it, is rich and multifaceted. Finally, bolstering everything is my innate motivation as a teacher and communicator to explain spiritual knowledge and principles in a way that allows more people to understand and consider them.

Because so much was revealed during our conversations, two or three of the women interviewed were concerned that they not be thought "crazy." This issue is humorously highlighted by a story Lucille Clifton told. In 1977, she was contacted by a set of consciousnesses who directed her to rise each morning and take down what they relayed to her about the condition of the world. For seven months, Lucille automatically transcribed what they channeled through her. During our interview, she mentioned that she was allowed to ask questions of them, but that now, looking back, she is appalled at how bad her questions were. Only once did she ask about something that she desired, and that was to inquire whether she could "do some interviews with dead poets. I would love that. I mean, this would be something I would like." Sometime later she received the answer that there were some poets who felt that would be "all right." However, when she wrote down the names, she discovered that Langston Hughes, the beloved Harlem poet, was not there:

> I said, "Well, where is Langston? I would like Langston."
> And then he [Langston] said, "Lucille, I do not want your friends to think you are crazy." Really. Because I did know him. He said that he thought people would have very odd ideas. He didn't want to be any part of this.

Although we probably laugh reading this, I hope Langston would have a very different response twenty-odd years later, when more and more openly people are talking to God, to beings from the Pleiades and Sirius, and other non-crazy people are reading and listening quite seriously to what they have to say.

In fact, over the past two decades, my perceptions about the current spiritual climate have been both fed and confirmed by an increasing spate of books now categorized by the publishing industry as "New Age," "Spirituality," and "Self-help." Avidly, I have read a good many of them—from important early works such as physicist Gary Zukav's *The Dancing Wu Li Masters,* naturalist Machaelle Small Wright's *Behaving As If the God in All Life Matters,* and Yoruba priestess Luisah Teish's *Jambalaya: The Natural Woman's Book of Personal Charms and Practical Rituals,* to more recent titles including: James Redfield's *The Celestine Prophecy; The*

Tibetan Book of Living and Dying; Julia Cameron's *The Artist's Way: A Spiritual Path to Higher Creativity;* Iyanla Vanzant's *Tapping the Power Within: A Path to Self-Empowerment for Black Women;* Joyce Elaine Noll's *Company of Prophets: African American Psychics, Healers and Visionaries;* Caroline Myss's *Anatomy of the Spirit: The Seven Stages of Power and Healing;* Malidoma Patrice Somé's *Of Water and the Spirit: Ritual, Magic, and Initiation in the Life of an African Shaman;* Arthur Zajonc's *Catching the Light: The Entwined History of Light and Mind;* Gloria Wade-Gayles's *My Soul Is a Witness: African American Women's Spirituality;* and Richard Carlson's *Don't Sweat the Small Stuff . . . and it's all small stuff;* to name just a few.

What I am working with now, my immediate spiritual and self-help "bibles," are: *Transforming the Mind: Teachings on Generating Compassion* by His Holiness the Dalai Lama; *Clear Your Clutter with Feng Shui* by Karen Kingston; *The Fear Book: Facing Fear Once and for All* by Cheri Huber; and *A Year to Live: How to Live this Year As If It Were Your Last* by Stephen Levine.

Into this New Age welter of words about spiritual transformation, *Soul Talk* must find its niche. To borrow a phrase from Michele Gibbs, this book is the "full-scale intervention" I can make at the present time. When I set foot on the path toward realized spirituality around 1980, the desire that propelled me with ever-increasing urgency was the need to know my true work in this world, what I personally and specifically was put here for, what I was supposed to do, what was the way, the calling, the cause that would make me feel justified. Without negating whatever of value I have done in the interim, I would say now that, for myself, *Soul Talk* has become a huge part of the answer.

≈1≈

THE THIRD REVOLUTION:
A New Spirituality Arises

Viewed from an inner, spiritual perspective, the late 1970s through the 1980s was a time of burgeoning transformation for humankind. On the external front, however, social and political conditions were dreadful. During the years that Ronald Reagan was president (1980–1988) domestic programs such as Medicare, federally funded student loans, summer youth employment, federally funded daycare, and welfare were drastically cut; taxes were minimally reduced for the poor and radically slashed for corporations and the wealthy; the federal government slackened its oversight of the banking industry, the natural gas industry, environmental protection, and voting and civil rights; military spending rose and the national debt soared; regressive communist scare tactics were employed to justify armed U.S. intervention in Nicaragua, El Salvador, and Grenada; the Ku Klux Klan began calling upon "white anger" as a response to busing and affirmative action. It was the period of the Savings and Loan crisis, the Iran-Contra affair, ketchup as a school lunch vegetable, and Reagan's own vilification of black mothers on Aid to Families with Dependent Children (AFDC) as "welfare queens." Seen from the outside, the picture was rather bleak.

Spiritual vision, however, mandates seeing from within as well as without, and from this viewpoint another scene emerges to balance all that was disheartening. In personal relations, science, work, education, religion, and medicine, people were evolving entirely new ways of being and seeing that sought to foster not just ameliorative measures but foundational change. Though they were discipline- and content-specific, these ways entailed leaps from accepted old material paradigms into expansive and spiritually based possibilities. Thus were born the multiplicity of discoveries, activities, and attitudes that were popularly and collectively tagged "New Age"—ranging from research in quantum physics that sought to prove mysterious, interpenetrating energies of the universe, to the employment by ordinary individuals of visualization for enhanced health, wealth, and success. On the surface, this New Age activity looked like a movement without much specific racial or gender content (since the "norm" of whiteness goes unremarked) and black women, in particular, were not very visible in it. But this was far from the reality.

Around 1980 an outburst of spirituality concomitantly erupted among African American women, just when the civil rights movement and the early ferment of the feminist movement were subsiding. This upsurge of spirituality continued from the wave of these two political movements and rippled forward as an extension of them. At the time, many concerned individuals were wondering what had happened to the energy needed to propel social change. We can now see that this transformative energy was moving to encompass spirituality in a deeper, explicit way, as preparation for grappling with social issues on a more profound level.

Black women embraced practices associated with the New Age, such as crystal work, Eastern religions, and metaphysics, and laid them alongside more traditional, culturally derived religious and spiritual foundations. The results could be seen in dramatic changes of lifestyle and life direction for many, and—even more visibly—in the remarkable outpouring of creative writing by authors such as Toni Morrison, Toni Cade Bambara, and Alice Walker, authors whose writing captured unprecedented public attention because of its blend of racial-feminist-political realism and spiritual-supernatural awareness. What African American women were creating added political dimension to the generally apolitical spiritual movement and contributed immensely to a higher collective spiritual consciousness.

Clearing Out, Moving (With)In

In my case, the shift toward spirituality around 1980 involved a physical move from one place to another. After seven years of teaching literature as my first real job at the University of Delaware and carving out a specialization in African American writing, I decided to spend the 1979–1980 year on sabbatical leave in the exciting city of Washington, D.C. (as compared to Newark, Delaware, college town), conducting scholarly research and having a good time. I had participated in the black power movement as a young graduate student, wife, and mother wholly supportive of the cause in academic and personal ways but not directly active. As a black feminist, I had been more central—generating theory and articles and working as a member of the Combahee River Collective Retreat Group, an association of fifteen to twenty African American women committed to consciousness-raising and organizing.

After I moved to Washington, D.C., the territory my own consciousness covered vastly expanded. At once, I connected with Konda, a dreadlocked sister from the west coast who was managing up-and-coming women's musical groups and fashioning for herself an alternative, black-culture-based style of living. I vividly remember walking down Columbia Road with her on a mid-August afternoon. It was hot and muggy, as Washington, D.C., can be, but I was internally fanned and exhilarated by the sounds, the energy, the international medley of dark, familiar faces.

When we stepped inside a store for something cool to drink, she bought a small bottle of apple juice. I came out with a grape "Icee," one of those sugar-water, artificial-color confections in a plastic sleeve with absolutely no redeeming nutritional value. As I happily slurped it up, Konda turned smiling and serious to me and said—out of the clear blue nowhere, "If you stop eating sugar and junk like that and stuff from cans, I bet you your skin will clear up." The right force of what she said and how she said it somehow kept me from being either shocked or offended. Thus, easy and simple as that, I began a train of changes leading to the eventual clearing up of much more than my acned skin, which had continued its distressing eruptions long past the years when first one dermatologist and then another had promised me it would smooth.

I did, indeed, "go off" sugar, processed foods, meat, and caffeine, the latter being difficult enough to teach me the little that I know about substance addiction and withdrawal. I gave up even the respectability of my short Afro and began growing dreadlocks—

in those days when they were not socially acceptable, not available "bottled" in hip beauty shops, not twisted into instant glamour by limber-fingered technicians who "do" locks. I traveled to the black Caribbean. All these were external indications of deep internal change that pushed me to ask with increasing urgency to be shown my true work in this world. What was I put here for? What was I *supposed* to do? What was the way, the calling, the cause that would make me feel, as Aretha Franklin put it, "justified"? This questioning arose, I see now, from a profound urge toward spiritual identity and meaning.

My religious life and my spiritual self were not subjects I had been thinking about. The childhood years I spent walking up the Norma Street hill to attend the Zion Baptist Church in Shreveport, Louisiana, had fizzled into coerced appearances as a young adult at the mandatory Sunday chapel of my undergraduate alma mater, Southern University, and had finally petered out altogether amidst the alien atmosphere of northern, white, academic institutions, where any possible "down-home" black churches or black people had to be painstakingly sought beyond hallowed, ivy walls. In the process of wresting from this unfamiliar system its sheepskins of validation, I shed a way of being spiritual in the world that I had always inhabited. However, both the former habitation and the shedding had taken place without considered thought or conscious choice. In 1979 my most overtly spiritual practices included saying grace at communal meals and holding hands with other women in feminist full moon circles. Maybe I prayed during desperate hours, maybe currents of language-less, thought-less faith coursed through me—but, for all intents and purposes, I had no active, deeply accessed spiritual life.

I began avidly reading popularly focused metaphysical books and articles. Many of these were current New Age titles, and quite a few were feminist-oriented. What comes most readily to mind are Jane Roberts's *The Education of Oversoul Seven;* Gary Zukav's *The Dancing Wu Li Masters;* an early twentieth-century "prosperity" author whose name I cannot remember; Migene G. Whippler's *Santeria;* Diane Mariechild's *Mother Wit;* Ann Farraday and Jungian-Senoi texts about dreams; and pamphlets and articles that turned me on to mind-body-spirit truisms and material about auras, Kirlian photography, the Tarot, astrology, Zen thinking, supernatural phenomena, the "secret life of plants," crystals, and synchronicity.

Because I was at the core a spiritually receptive, even hungry, individual, the avenues to transpersonal meaning and interconnection represented by all this reading strongly appealed to my intellect and emotions. The multiple, overlapping realities of Roberts's fable about a time-and-space-hopping supersoul intuitively struck me as accurate, and yes, it made sense that real need coupled with focused attention would make money appear, and that, in general, the universe was a wondrously mysterious but ordered and purposeful organism that could be read and entered into through any number of systems and means.

Except for Whippler's work on the African-Catholic syncretism that is Santeria, none of us would think to call any of this material "black." In fact, all of the authors are white, and the material itself is apparently raceless, that is, devoid of racial reference or implications. And it is raceless—in that the energy that is the universe, that takes form in us and in everything that exists cannot itself be regarded as raced (or sexed, or gendered, or, for that matter, anything else that happens when it reaches the dense physical plane of everyday life). And, yes, this New Age material is raceless in that every kind of people dreams, suffers, and rejoices under the same progression of planets and stars, and each and every person benefits from maintaining a peaceful and present mind. Yet, it is significant that in Washington, D.C., in 1980, a group of diverse black women including myself were passing around among ourselves Jane Roberts's *Oversoul Seven,* and that our friend Crystal was invoking some sorely needed, concrete prosperity to pay the rent and buy food for her child. This adds race—as it should be—to the picture of the emerging New Age. Spiritual wisdom and timeless principles, when run through African American women, tend to emerge with a different slant.

Toni Cade Bambara's novel *The Salt Eaters* provides the perfect means to illustrate this point. An altogether unprecedented and original act of creativity, this book is simultaneously New Age, female, *and* black. Published in 1980, the novel brought blazingly into focus the momentous happenings taking place in the consciousness of black women. *The Salt Eaters* tells the story of Velma Henry, an incredibly committed political activist in her forties who has attempted suicide and is undergoing a laying-on-of-hands healing by "the good woman" Ransom as a roomful of people look on. Velma has marched until her feet and womb bled for civil rights. She has struggled with other progressive sisters in her community to make "showboating" male leaders less sexist and more truly responsive to the people's needs. She has traveled with a troupe of Third World feminists staging educational dramas. She has put her life on the line for a healthy environment and a pacifist world. Finally, though, overtaken by negativity and despair, she slashes her wrists and sticks her head in the gas of her kitchen oven. During the difficult healing, readers experience Velma spinning through muggy memories and multiple lifetimes.

The Salt Eaters firmly contextualizes Velma within her family and community, but Toni's familiarity with both science and the supernatural takes her story into worlds every bit as vast and mind-boggling as Jane Roberts's metaphysical fable. Here, in this book, in 1980, was all the spirituality I was learning—and then some—made into a literary work that was impeccable in its daunting breadth of knowledge, difficult but dazzling style, and unimpeachable racial and feminist politics. The healing of Velma through the laying-on-of-hands is, in itself, not new or particularly startling. Nor is the circle of hard-praying church people or even, perhaps, the healer's down-to-earth spirit guide. Though these might not be staples of black spirituality, neither would they be considered unusual ingredients.

What is different in this book is the profound and wholly respectful attention accorded to these more traditional racial aspects, as well as to astrology, past lives and reincarnation, Tarot cards, the metaphysical extensions of quantum physics, chakras and energy, Sufi tales, psychic telepathy, numerology, ancient black Egyptian wisdom traditions, Eastern philosophies of cosmic connectedness, and so forth—in short, an array of alternative knowledge systems founded on the belief that this visible "phenomenal" world is the external reflection of an underlying "noumenal" reality that can—and indeed, should—be tapped for the full and optimum functioning of life in material form. In other words, *The Salt Eaters* validated largely unknown or discredited (by black people and whites), *non*-rational ways of knowing—and promoted the idea that we will function more effectively if we use the unseen energy that surrounds us.

Even more radical in the novel is the fact that all of these spiritual modalities are rooted in African and African American traditions and characters, and are geared toward the elimination of racism and other forms of social injustice and abuse. The thrust of Toni's work has always been the healing of the (black) "nation"—in this case symbolized by the repair of Velma's fractured self and psyche. Only when that internal and external work has been accomplished is health possible on larger scales. Ultimately, not only will Velma be made whole, but so too must her community, nation, the world, and the universe. As Toni outlines it, spiritual wisdom is first and foremost a force for transforming social and political ills—and those ills wear the very specific faces of racism, poverty, gender inequality, rampant capitalism, ignorance, and so forth. This is what I mean when I say that spirituality run through black women comes out with a different slant. Unlike the other New Age reading I was doing, this novel addressed issues that defined my identity-reality and lay close to my heart.

Thrilled, challenged, and totally impressed (and also slightly overwhelmed) by both the politics and the spirituality of *The Salt Eaters,* I became determined to write about this book, a desire inspired by my need to respond to it and the urge to help others understand the work. While I felt my experience and vocabulary would enable me to discuss its politics, I was not as proficient in the wide-ranging spiritual-metaphysical ideas and practices so casually incorporated throughout the text. I knew enough to scratch the surface, enough to identify the critical places at which to dig. But the novel's holistic spiritual command forced me to consult even more ancient and esoteric documents, pushing me into such areas as cosmic symbolism, grimoires, medieval magical texts, and the writing of Mme. Blavatsky, the famous theosophist and author of *The Secret Doctrine.*

Because it was within the context of late twentieth-century New Age culture that I discovered the spiritual truths underlying *The Salt Eaters,* that context was my immediate point of reference. Not so for Toni. She has always said that everything necessary for African American well-being exists within the black community—and this includes spiritual knowledge of any sort. Even the most esoteric learning she finds stored in the aunts and uncles, grandmothers and fathers who live in the neighborhood.

Years later as I spoke with Toni about this most challenging of her literary creations, I questioned her about where she, as the narrator, and the characters learned their spiritual knowledge—in particular, the genius Campbell (who I believe is Toni's alter ego or psychic double), a character in *The Salt Eaters* who can synthesize in one breathy sweep "voodoo, thermodynamics, I Ching, astrology, numerology, alchemy, metaphysics, everybody's ancient myths." What, I wanted to know, would she counsel an uninitiated person to do who desired to become as wise?

In response, she rattled out a string of resources and individuals including workshops with the black actress Barbara O., who played Yellow Mary in Julie Dash's film *Daughters of the Dust;* a black female university dean who can levitate; black "healing and light" temples, homeopathic clinics, and bookstores "in your neighborhood"; Luisah Teish's *Jambalaya;* three weeks of study in New Orleans with a practitioner "in the business" or the voodoo festival in Galveston or Alabama during the summer solstice; Odunde ceremonies in Philadelphia and New York City for our African ancestors; all the other "stuff" that goes on at the periphery of community observances such as Juneteenth or the Garvey Day parade. Incredulous, I said these would not enable anybody to know all that Campbell knows and that he had to have been reading New Age physics. Toni disagreed. She argued that Campbell "might have had an uncle who talks that talk," who might "lay out" the wisdom on top of his nephew's high school physics. Even though a lot of what was in the book came to *her* through reading, she was adamantly clear that "reading ain't going to get it."

This conversation left me feeling outside the kind of black community that Toni insisted existed. The closest thing I had to Campbell's uncle was a half-brother old enough to be my father, who mumbled drunken crypticisms about his Scottish Rite (mind you, not black Prince Hall) Masonic affiliation when I asked him relevant questions. And, although I stood with other displaced African sisters and brothers on the piers and prayed and tossed my offerings in the water, my presence at Odunde had not led me into any esoteric depths. Clearly, for Toni, growing up in Harlem in the late 1930s and 1940s had been an unparalleled, rich, Afrocentric cradling—especially given who she was and given her mother's revolutionary black nationalist politics—that would forever enable her to access the "black" at the heart of things.

I wondered if that world and others similar to it still flourished. I knew they did not for me or for many other African Americans of my generation and upbringing. I also acknowledged that reading alone did not "do it," but knew that for many of us it functioned as a huge resource. I wondered whether Toni was romanticizing. I never asked her this question outright. I knew she may have been doing in life what she does in her fiction, that is, sometimes painting black larger than life so that we will become visible in all our glory to ourselves and to the blind, negating white world. But she simply enlarges and highlights, never lies—so her basic premises still had to be taken as factual truths.

If I did not know exactly where to go with these matters years later, I certainly did not have the insight to even divine the issues in this way in 1980. Then, I held on to my copies of Idries Shah's tales of the mullah Nasrudin, pored through dictionaries of occult symbolism, read all the poorly printed pamphlets about healing the body that slumped on the back-aisle racks in dedicated health food stores, as well as Viktoras Kulvinskas's 1975 planetary healers manual, *Survival into the Twenty-first Century* (which my copy tells me I acquired in Washington, D.C., in 1979).

An indispensable resource in this enterprise was my then-partner Martha T. Zingo, who freely shared her rich occult library and her own extensive learning. Eternally my friend, this white, Italian-Irish-American working-class woman has always kept me spiritually and politically honest, never letting me forget that, even as I tended toward constructing seamlessly interlocked black-on-black narratives, she and other white women—some teachers, some important friends and lovers—have helped, like Toni's "muse" Khufu, to "pick the rocks up" out of my own and other black women's paths. With assistance from sources both here (acknowledged) and beyond (mostly unrecognized), I completed *The Salt Eaters* essay in an affirmed and solitary glow in 1981, sitting on the living room floor of our Northwest apartment. It is clear to me now that my heady foray into understanding Toni's work became the originating point for this present book. What I felt then was a strange, unnameable sense of having tapped into something bigger than myself that, through my expression, I had somehow helped to further.

Black Women Changing

Many other black women tell different yet similar stories of shifts and breakthroughs occurring around 1980. Michele Gibbs, a writer-artist-activist, recollects:

> Interesting—the period that you started noticing this shift in our [black women's] expression—because 1980 was a very pivotal year for me specifically. It marked the end objectively and also subjectively of long years of commitment to a certain way of inducing change, which is to say as a traditional community organizer with a very materially based approach to reaching people. And also in connection with that, I had finally concluded that not only was that particular method lacking, but that the context that I was living in was not very healthy for me, that context being the United States. That was the year I moved to Grenada.

From the day Michele set foot on the island, one extraordinary experience after another bore out her initial feeling that "this is the place I always dreamed I was from." Her father had died on March 13, 1961, the date of the Grenadian revolution. She traveled to the country to participate in Maurice Bishop's New Jewel socialist movement, not thinking of any other specific connections she might have to the place. From meeting a cab driver, however, who recognized her as a Gibbs because she "looked like all the rest of them around here," Michele discovered a family she had not known existed from the second leg of the triangular slave trade.

Events such as this, Michele says, "opened up a new way of seeing and being that I had buried within myself for many years, because as children, of course, we're open to all these things." Her father, a black American, and her mother, a white Jewish American, were both avowed and active Marxists. Growing up as the daughter of an interracial communist couple in Chicago during the early 1950s, she had lived in the few places that would rent to the family—in storefronts where "the only other people as bad off were gypsies, who very often lived next door." Although they were communists, her parents were "very clear that the best lesson they could teach me was not which line to follow, but how to think for myself." Adhering to their lead, she tried to expose herself to everything. Her family did not attend church, but she pursued her inner "mystical direction" through reading Lao-tse (whom she discovered by sneaking into the adult section of the library) and through her attraction to the beauty of the gypsies and their palm reading. Yet that "strain" of "intuition" got buried the same way that her artwork did when she turned fourteen. That was the year her father died, after having just left the Communist Party for its "final-racist-straw" failure to recognize the Algerian situation as a war of national liberation. As Michele recalls,

> I felt at that moment responsible for taking up where he had left off, and so I put down my paintbrush and picked up my picket sign, and I put down my piano and picked up the guitar, and devoted myself to social activism and being "socially responsible."

That path—which coincided with the 1960s "rising tide of everything positive and new and renewing that we could imagine then"—continued until her decision in 1980 to radically alter her life. Everybody in Detroit, where she had worked and organized, accused her of "deserting the ship," to which she replied: "Not necessarily. It's a ship that's about to sink anyway, and I'm going to get off of it. Remember J. J. Jones's injunction that 'It's not the size of the ship that makes the wave; it's the motion of the ocean.'" When she and her husband moved to Grenada, she vaguely imagined the possibility of combining picket sign and paintbrush, guitar and piano, rather than having to give up one in preference for the other.

This binary opposition is, of course, the way that politics and spirituality have been conceptualized; they have been viewed as diametric extremes, locked in conflict one with the other. Michele admits that she fell prey to this straitjacketing way of thinking because, in her words, "that was the reality I inherited." It is also the legacy that unravels Velma in *The Salt Eaters*. She breaks down as a result of being solely political and relentlessly logical, and gets well when she comes into conscious possession of her spiritual being. This political-versus-spiritual problem is, in fact, what motivated Toni to write the novel:

> There is a split between the spiritual, psychic, and political forces in my community. . . . . It is a wasteful and dangerous split. The novel grew out of my attempt to fuse the seemingly separate frames of reference of the camps; it grew out of an interest in identifying bridges; it grew out of a compulsion to understand how the energies of this period will manifest themselves in the next decade.

For Michele, the combination of "spiritual consciousness in the people" combined with the "environment of social transformation" in Grenada in 1980 boded well for deconstructing this classic schizophrenia on both personal and community levels:

Almost every encounter with somebody was a "significant encounter" where you are talking on many levels at once. You'd say, or somebody would say something like, "Nothing is known," and someone else would say, "Everything is known, it's just a question of who knows it." And so the environment itself pressed me to break through some frontiers that I might not have had courage to pursue on my own.

This "incredibly intense" melding of the spiritual and political was shattered by Grenada's internal coup and the United States' 1983 invasion of the island. Devastated and "forced back on spiritual resources," Michele fled to Lesbos, another warm, pretty island, and a place "which had a both mythical and real history as a power place for women":

It was someplace where I knew the energy would be totally different, spiritual in its own way, but would give me the emotional space I needed to become centered again. And that took about two and a half years. It took me a year and a half just to stop being more in Grenada than where I actually physically was. I mean, like every night you close your eyes and you're back there again, you're really back there. You're not only back there the way it was, but you're back there in the present with what was happening. And, you close your eyes, you're on the bus on the same road, and you see what the U.S. presence has put in the place of what you remember. And you're there, you're just there.

This out-of-body existence was, to say the least, very hard on her, but after the two and a half years of healing on Lesbos, Michele re-emerged, ready to engage again with the Caribbean and the world.

※

Coming from quite different directions, Namonyah Soipan, a somewhat younger psychotherapist and global traveler, arrived at 1980 when she similarly experienced a marked solidification of gradually emergent changes. Namonyah had spent the first years of her life as an extremely sensitive young girl living in New Jersey. After having a traumatic childhood near-death experience, she became obsessed with the idea of death and fervently embraced a fire-and-brimstone fundamentalist Christianity. She adamantly maintained her faith despite confusion about how to love a god that she was supposed to fear, and was also puzzled about why the coming of the Holy Ghost—taught to be a blessing—triggered a scene filled with "punishment, screaming, shouting, people getting hurt and moving out of the way." After she became not just a baptized but a *saved* Christian at sixteen, she began "to preach and go into churches and proselytize to kids at school," still feeling afraid but thinking that, now that she was saved and doing some missionary work, her "back was covered" and she need not worry about God's wrath or retribution. The disturbing emotional dissonance within her became a cacophony when she was told that she could no longer dance (this was prohibited by many fundamentalist churches)—or even ski:

> Now this is when I began to understand the difference between being a spiritual being and being a religious being, because skiing was a spiritual experience for me.

So I said to them, "Wait a minute." When I'm up on that mountain, I mean thousands of feet because I was a serious skier—I wanted to be in the Olympics, but my parents would not support that because they didn't want me to be a ski bum, so I was into slalom racing—so I would be up at the very top, up to the clouds, and when I was up there I'm talking about being enraptured. When I was skiing I was so tuned in to everything. This is before I even got into spiritual. I would tell people that it was better than an orgasm. Skiing for me was that divine, that brilliant, that magnificent, that I couldn't compare it to anything, but it was spiritual. I wasn't using that word at the time, I just knew that it was incredible and I felt close to God. When they told me that I had to stop skiing, that's when I said, "Wait a minute, something's wrong here." Because when I'm up on that mountain, I'm praying. I do prayers up there to help me down safely and never take anything for granted, but not only to help me get down the slope safely but to thank God for all this beauty. So skiing to me was not just recreational. They tried to take that away from me and that's when I started questioning and realizing these are man's rules. Religion is about following the rules, but it's about following man-made rules, and I said, "I got to get out of this, because I'm not stopping skiing."

Whereupon, Namonyah let go of the fundamentalist church but not its teaching. She continued attending the family Baptist church and went off to Boston University the next year—still proselytizing, still talking about Jesus Christ and cajoling her

Japanese roommate to accompany her to services. Her aunt's warning that philosophy would challenge her religious beliefs proved true, especially after she transferred to Antioch College in 1977 where, in that more experiential setting, she came into contact with transcendental meditation, parapsychology, and a friend whom she considered a sinner who exposed her to Tarot readings. Finally, in 1980, back in New York City, she met Konda (the same unique woman I had encountered the year before), who helped her open up to the intense spirituality that had simmered inside her. Konda introduced her to yoga and to setting up an altar and, as Namonyah describes it,

> That's my first conscious glimpse at spirituality—even though I had glimpsed it years ago at fifteen when I was up on those mountains. So when Konda is talking to me now I have a frame of reference—the mountains. And, yes, it's making sense. "God is in myself." All right, I know this. This is very familiar to me. I said to her, "It's skiing." So all this is clicking.

Now, Namonyah's spiritual growth could accelerate because she realized that this spirituality is what had protected her from losing herself completely as she had journeyed through her religious trip. Thus, she discovered for herself one of the key understandings buttressing this incoming New Age—the distinction between religion and spirituality, that religion can be spiritual though not automatically, and that spirituality is a more inclusive consciousness that allows for exploration of many, even heterodox, avenues to the divine. Understanding the idea of God immanent made her aware, at an operative and active level, of her innate spiritual essence, that sense of self she had always been tapping into that was far greater than any dogma.

From that point of understanding God as immanent within herself, Namonyah rapidly opened up to diverse, broad possibilities, such as practicing Tibetan Buddhism and meditation, chanting, taking yoga, smoking marijuana, going to live in Jamaica, and just "opening up, opening up, opening up," devouring the African history that had been denied her, and studying Egyptology and learning about the ancient Egyptian kingdom of Kemet. Returning in 1982 from her first trip to Africa, where she lived with the Masai in Kenya and looked up the Falasha, the original black Hebrews, in Ethiopia, Namonyah found she had left light years behind her the person she had been at the beginning of 1980.

Masani Alexis DeVeaux is a writer and teacher who drew on these identities, as well as her religious background, to define black women's spirituality. Because of her own evolution, she understood as readily as Michele did what I was talking about when I asked about the year 1980. She began speaking about her own personal experience, but quickly catapulted to a larger perspective. Born into a Baptist family, she had religion in her life because she was "extraordinarily close" to her grandmother, whom she liked to watch wield her power as a member of the church's senior usher board. Even though she attended services because otherwise "Grammy" would withhold her allowance, she genuinely enjoyed the singing, children's programs where she recited poetry, and "the whole atmosphere."

It wasn't until she was in her early twenties that Masani Alexis rebelled, deeming church "too confining." At that point, in the early 1970s, she took off in other, less traditional directions. Eventually, she learned transcendental meditation, began studying with the Rosicrucians after responding to one of their magazine advertisements, extrapolated the Rosicrucian's emphasis on Egypt into Afro-ology, deeply explored the Yoruba religion—even wearing waist beads—but without ever wanting to become a priestess. She found and still finds it difficult to "join somebody else's thing," although she can draw from it, and she definitely cannot affiliate with anything "that's going to be anti-gay or anti-woman." Coming to the early 1980s, she incorporated tai chi, yoga, and "right eating," reaching a comfortable place that she now calls "the last major transformation of my spirituality," a convergence of different parts that has left her centered and no longer searching or, as she says, flitting around.

Masani Alexis is certain that the growth that she and her immediate milieu experienced was a breakthrough of global proportions. She expresses this certainty explicitly and enthusiastically:

> I think the thing about that period in the '80s in Brooklyn is that in our singular community—little small community that we were—we were beginning to really express black women's consciousness in a way that it had not been expressed. . . . When we come to the '80s, that consciousness was no longer in disguise. . . . And at the time that we threw the covers off, we were free to do and really become. Once that happened, everybody got big, every black woman got big. Every black woman was able to tap into every other black woman and was able to tap

into every black woman in history and to a channeling. This is what we did. . . . Even people who were not conscious did—even if they tapped into one person, even if they tapped into some black actress, even if they tapped into a black woman's magazine. . . . Not to mention those of us who were consciously tapping. We were *really* blowed up, you know. But we had all that going—Alice Walker, Toni Cade Bambara, Toni Morrison, all of them, all of us, all of that. All of that was stimulating consciousness, so there was no way we could not get big. . . . That consciousness could not be confined to the borders of North America. So then traveling connected us to that global consciousness; having a sense of the cultural experience of other women connected us to that global consciousness. Once we knew ourselves, we had to know the planet.

What I understand Masani Alexis to be saying here is that, around 1980, African American women began to have an enlarged sense of ourselves and the world. Ignited first by the movements of the 1960s and '70s that instilled racial and female pride, this sense of being "big," of "bigness," or psychic and social expansion, was further fed as we accessed our spiritual dimensions. She also implies that spiritual consciousness is a limitless force capable of crossing geographic and cultural barriers. No wonder, then, that travel beyond the United States figures so prominently in our stories, the physical action of travel being symbolic of large supra-physical change. As spiritual consciousness heightened on a planetary scale, African American women responded and contributed to that consciousness—a dynamic visible in the work and influence of the writers Masani mentions. This heightening of spiritual energy is, of course, also unmistakable in the way our life histories and patterns so sharply changed. Masani Alexis, Namonyah, Michele, and I had all adhered to certain systems of belief—whether the Baptist religion or, in Michele's case, a communist idealism that functioned as religion—which we grew to find inadequate, inconsequential, or confining. For all of us, 1980 was a turning point.

It was the year we each independently began exploring radically different spiritual teachings and paths, avenues that were less traditional for African American women and that brought us in confluence with the rapidly accreting New Age—even as we instinctively played out the realities of race and gender that defined us and gave shape and meaning to our lives. We read the usual New Age books and journals, sat before altars and meditated, rejected solely materialistic modes of existence, embraced yoga and tai chi and Buddhism—all common coin of the burgeoning New Age realm. However, we simultaneously applied our new learning to black subject matter, found spiritual transcendence in black revolutionary struggle, and sought metaphysical origins in Africa. Our consciousness as African American women worked on the new material and energies even as they worked on us, and the results were both customary and unique.

Finally, Masani Alexis's remark about connection to the "cultural experience of other women" is an important reminder that remarkable changes were also occurring among white women and other women of color. My favorite example of these collective and collaborative changes is the 1981 anthology edited by Cherríe Moraga and Gloria Anzaldúa, *This Bridge Called My Back:*

Writings by Radical Women of Color. Conceived in response to racism in the white women's movement, its goal was to reflect an uncompromised definition of feminism by women of color who were committed to radical revolution. The book discusses varied subjects including: the experience of growing up as dark children; racism in the women's movement; theory that accounts for the actual, concrete realities of those who live in female bodies of color; culture, class, and homophobia; the third world woman writer; and sacred vision.

Notably, Toni Cade Bambara contributed a foreword to *This Bridge Called My Back* that speaks to the political and spiritual promise inherent in the kind of life-affirming work that the anthology represents. It began:

> How I cherish this collection of cables, esoesses, conjurations and fusile missiles. Its motive force. Its gathering-us-in-ness. Its midwifery of mutually wise understandings. Its promise of autonomy and community. And its pledge of an abundant life for us all. On time. That is to say— overdue, given the times. ("Arrogance rising, moon in oppression, sun in destruction"—Cameron)

From her position as an observant black woman, Toni concluded by looking forward to "the blueprints we will draw up of the new order we will make manifest."

Cosmic Consciousness Shifts

Change is definitely what this late 1970s–early 1980s period was all about. 1980 seems to have acted as a hinge, a moment on which the collective consciousness swung into a higher vibration, shifting toward more expanded planes of awareness and moving through available portals that initiated new modes of thought and behavior. Much occurred of historical, scientific, and artistic note, having begun years earlier with that marvelous, now near-fabulous, elongated decade that we in the United States call "the sixties." What was set in motion then took form and transformed, gathering substance and momentum until, by the early 1980s, the changes had assumed a definite enough shape that many attuned individuals began to register and name them. Marilyn Ferguson's 1980 study, *The Aquarian Conspiracy*, comes immediately to my mind.

In this "New Age watershed classic," as the book is described on its jacket, Ferguson gives both the details and broad trends of what the subtitle calls *Personal and Social Transformation in Our Time*. In the early 1970s, Ferguson conducted research about the brain and consciousness and encountered startling scientific and lay data regarding "accelerated learning, expanded awareness, the power of internal imagery for healing and problem solving, and the capacity to recover buried memories." All of her subsequent work further suggested that the social activism of the 1960s and the consciousness revolution of the 1970s "seemed to be moving toward an historic synthesis: social transformation resulting from personal transformation—change from the inside out." The characteristics and subtlety of this movement made her think of a conspiracy—in the sense of priest-scientist Pierre Teilhard de Chardin's "conspiracy of love" and in the root meaning of the word *conspiracy*, "to breathe together." In order to further "make clear the benevolent nature of this joining," Ferguson linked "conspiracy" with Aquarius, the zodiacal sign of the water bearer, "symbolizing flow and the quenching of an ancient thirst." She was also "drawn to" the cultural dream "that after a dark, violent age, the Piscean, we are entering a millennium of [Aquarian] love and light."

In one important chapter, Ferguson recounts how neuroscientist Karl Pribram and Einstein protégé David Bohm's discoveries led to the revolutionary theory that says "our brains mathematically construct 'hard' reality by interpreting frequencies from a dimension transcending time and space." This makes the brain a hologram—an organic, holistic, complete, self-perpetuating system where any piece contains the entire whole—interpreting a likewise holographic universe. Thus, each person participates in reality and affects what he or she observes. This theory, as Ferguson states, "establishes the supernatural as part of nature," since the dimension transcending time and space (the so-called supernatural) is translated into what we generally take to be natural, concrete reality.

> In this framework, psychic phenomena are only by-products of the simultaneous-everywhere matrix [this is the hologram]. Individual brains are bits of the greater hologram. They have access under certain circumstances to all the information in the total cybernetic system. Synchronicity—the web of coincidence that seems to have some higher purpose or connectedness—also fits in with the holographic model. Such meaningful coincidences derive from the purposeful, patterned, organizing nature of the matrix. Psychokinesis, mind affecting matter, may be a natural result of interaction at the primary level. The holographic model resolves one long-standing riddle

of psi [psychic phenomena]: the inability of instrumentation to track the apparent energy transfer in telepathy, healing, clairvoyance. If these events occur in a dimension transcending time and space, there is no need for energy to travel from here to there. As one researcher put it, "There isn't any *there*."

Or, there isn't any "out there." Leading up to this last quarter century, such breakthrough understandings in all fields of human endeavor were expanding consciousness by bridging the apparent duality between mind and matter, science and spirit. New innovative learning techniques assigned value to inner experience, imagery, dreams, and feelings; impeccably designed medical studies proved that patients who were prayed for—even by strangers—recovered faster than those who were not.

Ferguson's *The Aquarian Conspiracy* certainly captures powerfully and persuasively the "great shift of values" that was occurring throughout the world. But nowhere in her 450 pages does she discuss race or say anything at all about black women. In her seventh chapter on "Right Power," she purports to look at "experiments in social transformation," analyzing the transformative effects that "the protest and counterculture of the 1960s" had on both their participants and society at large. There is commentary here about Jerry Rubin and the Chicago Eight, the Communist party in southern California, New Left thinkers, VISTA and the Peace Corps, and the Students for a Democratic Society. But not a word about the civil rights or black power movements. And her section in this chapter on "The Power of Women" is color blind.

Ferguson's work in this book is heavily based on questionnaire data she received from 185 respondents, whom she describes as "a powerful network of leading-edge thinkers, businesspeople, scientists, and politicians who are working to create a different kind of society based on a vastly enlarged concept of human potential." The book's appendix summarizes information about these respondents, revealing where they live, their marital status, their gender, their political self-labeling, the spiritual disciplines and growth modalities instrumental for them, body therapies they have experienced, their positions on the validity of psychic phenomena, and so forth. But here, again, the reader learns nothing about their race. In this, Ferguson further evidences an insensitivity to race and an omission of race as a vitally necessary consideration—both of which have helped to give the "New Age" a bad name—further compounded, in some cases, by the careless appropriation of spiritual lore from traditions of color. Ferguson's premise is that, after the political and social agitation of the 1960s and 1970s, change was now beginning to occur, as she put it, more from the "inside out" than the outside in. Who could better illustrate this point than individuals such as the African American women discussed in this chapter, whose superbly articulated understanding of their lives encoded this paradigmatic shift?

As a black female reader I had to enter into the wealth of this very important and informative book accepting the (unstated) idea that the "personal and social transformation" it charted was something spiritual that transcended race, and therefore, expectations for representation of the embodied self and specific material issues had to be either consciously set aside or unconsciously blanked out of active awareness. Still, there were those of us who read this New Age material and subscribed to the exciting facts it presented—because we recognized their spiritual truth intuitively and within the changed parameters of our own lives. However, we clearly had to look elsewhere for images and information that mirrored who we were on every other level. Consider the following example.

In 1981, Toni Morrison appeared on the March 30 cover of *Newsweek* magazine. The bold caption read, "Black Magic," a clever but insensitive phrase that fed into racial stereotypes associating African-derived people with *black* magic, and subtly insinuating that anything so powerful as what Toni Morrison was doing (that had white people and the white establishment paying homage to her) must have been achieved via means beyond her own natural capability. Despite all this, the phrase accurately identified the very aspect of Morrison's and other black women's writing that was causing their work to fire the minds and hearts and imaginations of an unprecedented number of readers. Morrison and her sister writers were also "Aquarian conspirators"—attuned to the rays of cosmic change sweeping over us, and, beyond that, they were translating those energies into forms that revolutionized the people who touched them, causing "personal and social transformation in our time." In the same way as the respondents in Ferguson's book, these black women writers were moving beyond outmoded Piscean ways and into the future, breaking paradigms of the old rationality and spinning new spiritual models. And they were doing this in a way that helped make the transition accessible and acceptable to large numbers of people.

In the article, Morrison talks about her family experience— about her family telling ghost stories, her grandmother using a dream book to play the numbers, and her father having sometimes trickster-like communications with her after his death. She concludes, "We were intimate with the supernatural." Thus, it is not surprising that the world of her novels is filled with what the *Newsweek* editor Jean Strouse termed "signs, visitations, ways of knowing that reached beyond the five senses." Morrison's 1977 novel, *Song of Solomon,* offered up the character of a self-birthed root worker named Pilate who had no navel, roaming and protective ancestral ghosts, flying Africans imitated in their liberating "riding of the air" by their contemporary descendants, a woman named Circe who is as old as time—all set within a realistic here-and-now where the ravages of racism had yet to be battled on both internal and external fronts. Most of the outer weight of *Song of Solomon* is carried by the ostensible hero, Milkman, who embarks upon a journey through which he finds his true kin, roots, name, and self—and thus gains the knowledge and heart that will enable him to be a black man who can love and benefit his race. Pilate, his aunt, creates her starkly original existence outside societal norms, living in a shack with her daughter and granddaughter and selling homemade wine when they need cash money. She is the novel's living ancestral figure who conveys spiritual wisdom.

Tar Baby, Morrrison's work published in 1981, raised to uncommon heights the handling of nature and the natural environment. Her deft insight allows her to explore what it means to carry life-consciousness in non-human mineral and vegetable form in a striking manner—through ocean, fog, and trees—as she taps the psychic pain of two black people, a dark skinned, roots-culture man and a high-yellow woman of privilege, trying to love each other.

On the one hand, in Morrison's novels, we are presented with the hard realities of what it means to be raced black, and raced and gendered black female in a predominantly white—

predominantly white male—world. On the other, she validates everything that the New Age Aquarian theorists are positing about the naturalness of so-called supernatural phenomena and about our ability as spiritual human beings to function within these spaces. Her validation harks back to traditions of blackness that remind us that the New Age wisdom itself is not really new—only our enlarged capacity to accept, explain, appreciate, and benefit from it is fresh. Consequently, her unambiguous and unabashed handling of these subjects wraps us in enough traditional familiarity and inspires enough belief and courage to foster our incorporation of more daring but similar truths. The depiction of Pilate using the force of her intention to protect her unborn nephew is akin to and helps create the New Age climate where we powerfully enact our daily "affirmations" and think the "positive" thoughts that create our world.

Looking back at myself and other African American women I knew, and at the transformations Ferguson documents in *The Aquarian Conspiracy,* I can see now that, around 1980, many people's lives were humming—at higher frequencies—with a brand new music and that massive identity shifts were taking place. This phenomenon was definitely about something "spiritual," a word the black women I associated with started using to denote all the unseen avenues to power that enabled us to withstand the pernicious racism-sexism-classism-heterosexism of our daily existences. The benefit we derived from taking our religious-spiritual impulses to higher levels was the strength we garnered to walk this tainted Earth. We were part of a spiritual quickening that was sweeping the planet, an inspired imperative to pierce through the received, the material, and the limited obvious into the realm of invisible and divinely potentiating energies that give rise to the physical world—a motivation no more true for the physicists' probing construction of a holographic universe than for Morrison's fictional world—a world of ghosts that heal, Africans who fly, trees that talk, and women who make magic—or the spirit guides, mud mothers in a mirror, and revolution-talking drums of Toni Cade Bambara's *The Salt Eaters.*

TALKING TO ANCESTRAL LIGHT:
Communications from the Other Side

One of the strongest features of the new spirituality that arose in the early 1980s among African American women is its ancestral connectedness. For both traditional African and certain African American worldviews, being conversant with ghosts and spirits is not at all unusual and is, in fact, expected and often welcomed. Now that New Age physics and metaphysics posit the undying continuity of living energy, theory of this sort can be placed alongside the actual experience of generations. Further, a significant number of people are reporting conversations with out-of-body beings. Lucille Clifton, African American writer and mother, came into a surprising and rich relationship with her own deceased mother. The contact sparked a series of poems through which she told her story. Lucille's mother—representative of specific and collective ancestral lineage—appeared to her as light, as *spiritual* light. Through its telling, Lucille's story, too, emphasizes light as divine source and light as the fountainhead of her creativity. Interestingly, what Lucille came to know first-hand about the vast and purposeful multidimensionality of light as the essence of being is validated by both African shaman Malidoma Patrice Somé and physicist Arthur Zajonc in their studies of ritual and science.

Other African American women, too, speak about their experiences with ancestors. Without fail, the communication is beneficent, soothing, comforting, and inspirational, and it reminds us of the physical and psychic ways that calling on ancestors has always empowered African American struggle in the world. Now, the black cultural lore about departed spirits can be viewed with increased sophistication and shared with greater openness than ever before. Furthermore, what is occurring among black women becomes an aspect of how New Age energies are bringing all of us into ever closer rapport with the astral realm, that spiritual plane lying just beyond the physical world.

"In Populated Air/Our Ancestors Continue"

Lucille Clifton's communication with her dead mother began one afternoon in 1975 when she and her two eldest daughters—then sixteen and fourteen years old—were sitting idly at home while her four younger children napped. After rejecting an outing at the movies, they pulled down the Ouija board from the closet where they stored the family games. It was something they had played with only casually before, from which they had gotten only "foolishness." Her eldest daughter said that she would record the message; Lucille and her younger daughter would put their hands on the board. When it began moving—faster than it ever had before—Lucille exclaimed to her younger daughter, who answered, "Ma, I'm not doing that, *you're* doing it." Lucille said she wasn't and asked the board emphatically, "Who is it?" It responded "T . . . H," at which point Lucille and her daughter removed their hands. When they tried again—this time with their eyes closed—it spelled out "THELMA." Absolutely skeptical, Clifton put the board away. A few days later, they took it down again, with Lucille challenging, "Now, this is not funny. What is happening here?" The energy answered, spelling out "IT'S ME BABY. . . DON'T WORRY ABOUT IT . . . GET SOME REST," and the planchette dashed off the board.

Both Lucille and her daughters recognized THELMA as Lucille's mother, Thelma Moore Sayles, who had died one month before Lucille's first child was born. This unsought, unexpected supernatural contact with her mother inaugurated Lucille's conscious recognition of the spiritual realm. At this point, she was thirty-eight years old and married, with six children: "And I wasn't into a thing of wanting my mother, because by this time, when people said 'Mother' they were talking about *me*."

Because Lucille does not "believe things as easily as one might think," she was able to accept her communication with her mother only after her mother had continued to reappear. Eventually, she could tell by the feel of the spirit that it was definitely her mother: "You can distinguish. . . . You know if you're in a room with someone. There's a different feeling with different people." She once asked, "What are you? Have you crossed the void? Are you in the great beyond? Have you traversed the universe?"—using every high-flown euphemism she could think of—and her mother answered flatly, *I'm dead.* "Dead!" Lucille replied. "That's cold." She began reading about such spiritual phenomena, seeking information and precedents about being in active relationship with the spirit world.

Over a period of time, all six of her children would see Thelma and have experiences of some sort with her. Lucille began to address Thelma as Greta because "in spirit she said that she was once a woman named Greta and she liked that life very much, and so she'd prefer to be called Greta. The life of Thelma she wasn't crazy about, and I could see why." Lucille believed this was due to Thelma's seizures and her husband's philandering. Lucille's children's experiences with their deceased grandmother often involved a kind of care or concern. Thelma-Greta would, for instance, come to Lucille and get her to call her youngest son, and then she would say to Lucille: *Tell him to tell you what he did at Kevin's house.* Of course, her son felt totally aggrieved at this surveillance and complained, "Why is she always watching me? Why doesn't she watch—[some other sibling]?" On another occasion, Lucille's oldest daughter was coming down the steps carrying a too-large box of records in her arms. She tilted forward, beginning to fall—when everyone at the bottom of the stairs "watching this phenomenon" saw her suddenly tip back upright. Thelma said, *We're not in the business of keeping people from what happens to them. . . but she would have hurt herself bad.*

When these contacts with the spirit of her mother began, Lucille was afraid she was "cracking up. I thought, 'I'm going crazy and I'm taking my kids with me.' That's a big drag, because I wouldn't do that. If I was going, I probably wouldn't take my children." Finally, Lucille says, she came to believe, and even her children began to know this dead grandmother better than they knew their father's mother, who was still alive and living in Wilmington, North Carolina.

Lucille says that after the Ouija board episode she began "feeling itchy" in her hand. She also started doing what she called "listening/hearing," and the idea came to her that she should try writing. When she did, she received automatic messages faster. On one occasion, her pen wrote: *Stop this. You're having conversations with me as if I'm alive. I am not alive. Go. Conversation is for live people.* At one point, she asked why she was receiving such communication, and her mother replied, *You are a natural channel.* In the mid-1970s, nobody—to Lucille's knowledge—was saying the word "channel." (And about this, her family also joked, the kids teasing, "Ma's a canal.") Later, when people began using the term, she thought how interesting it was that that was her mother's word. And she knows that this language was not something that she had read or absorbed anyplace other than where it came from—through her mother.

From time to time, Thelma imparted various bits of information and advice. One of her "sayings" has been very helpful to Lucille. Thelma once said, *Baby, you might trip, but you will not fall.* That reminder has helped Lucille to have faith in the universe. Lucille also conjectures that, perhaps because she sees it as "not threatening," the universe does not threaten her:

> I think energy does work that way. Fear is a great blocker
> of energy. I have been afraid and I know. I've seen my-
> self immobile with fear. That energy is real, just like this
> table. Any physicist will tell you that. We don't have to
> deal with metaphysics about that. So energy doesn't dis-

solve. Science knows that. So the energy that is those who have left their flesh is still around.

Communication with the physically dead is very much a part of African and African American culture. In traditional African thought, for as many as four generations the dead continue to visit with family and friends who knew them when they were alive. They give advice, regulate behavior, and, most important, act as intermediaries between the world of God and the human realm. Significantly, Lucille's first word from her mother was Thelma's announcement of her name. The calling of the departed one's name helps to keep him or her "alive" in the human world. When no one remembers the dead person by name, they then totally cross over into the spirit dimension, dropping out of the realm of time and the present into all-consuming timelessness.

So it is not surprising that Thelma would appear to her daughter, Lucille. But how she chose to do so is very interesting. There is something almost comic about her coming via the Ouija board, the name of which comes from combining the French word *oui*, meaning "yes," and the German word *ja*, meaning "yes." Ouija, a method of spirit communication which uses an alphabet-printed board and a planchette, was invented as such in the United States in the mid-nineteenth century. It became widely popularized during the 1960s as a Parker Brothers game. Though its antecedent roots may reach back to Egypt, its being in Lucille's closet was a decidedly American, decidedly New Age-related thing. Lucille's attunement to spiritual energies is further shown in the way she combines physics and metaphysics to explain as natural and scientific what is usually considered supernatural, that is, the presence of ghosts. Her explanation couches her understanding of her mother's presence in a sophisticated technical language unavailable to black women of earlier times.

Wanting to better understand how contact between them was able to happen at all, Lucille once asked her mother, "So, when I call you, do you just come? Mom, are you watching me all the time?"—to which Thelma replied, *Well, Baby, you are not that interesting.* Lucille confesses that she was put out by this response because she thought she was "quite interesting." And she very correctly concludes about Thelma: "See, it's not like the woman is trying to please me at all. She's quite the same as she always was, actually." For Lucille, some of the things Thelma manages to do seem motivated more by Thelma's desires than by those of the living. For example, a male colleague of Lucille at St. Mary's College calls on Thelma to get parking places and, Lucille adds, "She's very good about it." His requests to Thelma had begun because he had seen Lucille do this and she had explained, "Well, my mother will get us a parking space if we just ask her. I mean, she's not going to read our minds." So, now, her colleague will go someplace and say, "Thelma, this is M.—I need a parking place." Then he'll drive around the block again and somebody will pull out and give him a space. Lucille guesses that, because Thelma could not drive in life, doing this is somehow fun for her.

When Lucille inquired of Thelma, with regard to supernormal powers, "Is there anything that I can do that's interesting?" her mother told her two things. The first was, *You can touch people and then you'll feel something about them*—which she trusts, although "sometimes nothing happens." The second was that she could *tell the truth* by simply asking to do so, shutting off her own thoughts and senses, and then saying the words that come out of her mouth. Now, Lucille reads palms, casts horoscopes, bestows blessings when requested, and generally continues to negotiate the world as a two-headed woman, that is, one who possesses magical power, who can see what is here and visible as well as that which is beyond ordinary vision.

She is singularly matter-of-fact about her gifts. "Being special," she avers, "has absolutely nothing to do with anything" and is, in fact, "defeating." At particularly magnetic poetry readings, when the audience was moved to radical action, she has sometimes thought that she could be "dangerous." But it takes her only five minutes, she laughs, to remember that she is actually the person who still cannot program her VCR: "So, how important and interesting could I be?" Speaking more soberly, Lucille reveals that basically what she feels is "lucky" and, paradoxically, that "it's a mixed blessing—because sometimes I might get information that I don't want to have." And, besides, she maintains, whatever abilities she holds "might be gone tomorrow. I don't know." In the face of these unusual occurrences, she remains rooted, earthy, solidly grounded—just as countless African American women before her, even when they could not reason through their gifts and experiences.

Lucille's communications with her mother have slackened in recent years. (Lucille believes she is about to be reborn.) However, she turned into a series of poems the initial contact that occurred between the two of them. When Lucille is speaking and recounts her spiritual reunion with her mother, she does so with humor and equanimity. By contrast, the voice in her poems reveals a sense of turmoil and trouble that her humorous, oral retelling does not even begin to touch.

Both the written and spoken versions of Lucille's experience present the same basic story. They tell about a time in her life when "a shift of knowing" made possible the breakthrough to higher levels of awareness and personal power. This is the kind of personal, spiritual breakthrough that I consider characteristic of the period around 1980. It is not surprising to me that these poems were published in that year in her volume entitled *two-headed woman*. Groping for an explanation for what is happening to her, Lucille finally hits upon the right "perhaps" in these four lines:

> *or perhaps*
> *in the palace of time*
> *our lives are a circular stair*
> *and i am turning*

This statement reveals her knowledge that time does not move in a linear, lockstep march. At this point, the turning, the metamorphosis she is about to effect, is awesome because it supersedes what the Rastafarians call "earth runnings" for a more divine and cosmic dimension. This process (and process it is) involves a crisis of belief, but it leads finally to new and certain knowledge.

Lucille heralds the change in a prefatory poem entitled "the light that came to lucille clifton," in which she uses her own real name to speak from heart and brain about herself. She talks about her shifting summer, "when even her fondest sureties / faded away" and she "could see the peril of an / unexamined life." However, she closed her eyes, "afraid to look for her / authenticity," but "a voice from the nondead past started talking." As she states in the poem:

> *she closed her ears and it spelled out in her hand*
> *"you might as well answer the door, my child,*
> *the truth is furiously knocking."*

Here, the phrase "spelled out in her hand" is a reference to one of her automatic writing experiences.

Subsequently, in the main sequence of the poems, Lucille begins her story about seeing her dead mother. Casting herself as a deponent in a civil and ecclesiastical court, using religious and legal language (and, again, her full legal name) she "hereby testifies" that, in a room alone, she saw a light and heard the sigh of a voice which contained another world. Asking in the next poem, "who are these strangers / peopling this light?" she is told, "lucille / we are / the Light." Understandably, the following poem begins, "mother, i am mad":

> someone calling itself Light
> has opened my inside. . . .
> someone of it is answering to
> your name.

Then ensue "perhaps" and possible "explanations." Friends come and try to convince her that she is losing her mind. But she is able to say to them:

> friends
> the ones who talk to me
> their words thin as wire
> their chorus fine as crystal
> their truth direct as stone,
> they are present as air.
>
> they are there.

As an ordinary woman who has not even dreamed of receiving visitations from unearthly places, Lucille finds her sanity and faith sorely tested. Prior to encountering her dead mother, she was comfortable with the female realities of sex and childbirth. Suddenly she is beset by angels, and Mary, and metaphysical speculation regarding the nature of the universe. She tries to run from the "surprising presence" with which she has been confronted, but "the angels stream" before her, "like a torch." There is no escape. Thus, the final, quiet poem sounds like a reprise or a coda:

> in populated air
> our ancestors continue.
> i have seen them.
> i have heard
> their shimmering voices
> singing.

While all of our ancestors—whether black, white, brown, red, or yellow—continue to exist in ethereal, akashic air, in this series of powerful poems, Lucille documents her own, specific connection with black female ancestral spirit, narrating her frightening but ultimately enlightening contact with her deceased mother. Blessed with the dual vision of a two-headed woman, blessed as a creative artist, she is able to affirm through her writing an experience that has characterized the spirituality of many African American women, but about which they have not been able to speak so openly and wonderfully. That Lucille first channels her mother and not some ascended master puts the whole experience on common ground. The messages, too, are not cosmically elevated, but funny and down-to-earth, eminently suited for a woman like Thelma's daughter, someone whose needs are basic: rest, self-knowledge, and an occasional parking space. In the same way that many women's spirituality differs from many men's in being rooted and unpretentious, these brushes with spirit are tied to the body and the everyday. Thus, all of us contemporary seekers are taught that the spiritual can wear a humanly congenial face.

Ancestral Light, Creative Life

Lucille's pivotal contact with her deceased mother was, for her, an experience of light. She spoke of it as "the light that came to lucille clifton" and of her mother and the other beings whom she saw as "strangers / peopling this light" who were in fact "the Light." It makes perfect sense that Lucille's initiation into direct knowledge of the spiritual world would be into light since that is what spirit seems to be. When pure spirit, unmanifested life, touches and informs matter or primordial substance, then and only then does something appear that can be seen, making vision possible. This something is light rendered as color.

In his fascinating book *Catching the Light*, physicist and metaphysicist Arthur Zajonc describes how, when viewed through a prism, colors appear where light meets dark, and he further demonstrates how light only reveals itself where there is an object to reflect it. His deepest studies into light at the quantum level, the photon, show it to be indivisible, its most "fundamental feature" being not smallness but "wholeness." Zajonc concludes that, essentially, light itself is non-sensory, is spiritual, just as was the immaterial energy of Lucille's mother. He states:

> Seeing light is a metaphor for seeing the invisible in the visible, for detecting the fragile imaginal garment that holds our planet and all existence together. Once we have learned to see light, surely everything else will follow.

"Seeing the invisible in the visible" is yet one more way of articulating the dual vision that Lucille and other wise ones possess. This faculty could also be spoken of as seeing the extraordinary in the ordinary, the divine in the human, the hidden in the obvious, the noumenal in the phenomenal—and vice versa. When Lucille once asked, "What is God?" she says that she was told, *God is Love, is Light, is God.* She continues:

> "God" isn't something that I particularly say because it's too externally defined. So I talk about the Universe. But for me the Universe is like Light, big "L." And I believe in that. I believe that there is a Light. . . . It's like the making clear what has not been clear, the being able to see what has not been seen. I think I just feel instinctive trust in that.

Here it is quite apparent that Lucille's intuitive understanding grasps the same theory that Zajonc's quantum physics posits. The spark of light divine is what all life appears to have in common, what connects individual bits of light-life to their source and to all else that exists in the four phenomenal kingdoms—mineral, vegetable, animal, human—and to the supra-human realms. Interestingly, the name "Lucille," means light. Although her family had planned to name her Georgia, after both of her grandmothers, when her father saw her "so pretty," he changed the name to Lucille. It connects her to the concept of light, and also to the Dahomean great-great-grandmother—named Lucy in America—who stands farthest at the known head of her family line. And this revered ancestor, in turn, links Lucille back to the richness of the wisdom traditions practiced for centuries by indigenous African peoples.

For example, in the remarkable book *Of Water and the Spirit,* one initiation that the author—contemporary African shaman Malidoma Patrice Somé—narrates takes the ritual mastery of light back to generations-old practices of his West African Dagara people. Yet, while he rests on ancestral roots, he renders the knowledge with the kind of flawless scientific and spiritual precision that so powerfully brings it into the postmodern world. A particular part of the initiation ceremony transported the initiates into the world of the soul through a hole of light. Having jumped in, Malidoma slowly begins to register the light as "a symphony of luminescent wires, all in motion and breathing life." He must grab one of them to anchor himself and, having done so, he notices that the strands he holds "were a live bundle in which tiny cells of changing colors moved slowly upward within what looked like a thin tube of translucent glass. Each cell twinkled. They were alive—and so was the whole bundle. Each cell lived as a whole within a whole."

As "an invisible presence bathing in the light" of his invisibility—visible, that is, only to his own consciousness—he experiences the powerful presence of the light. He becomes aware of motion, and describes the sensation as feeling "as if a consciousness or a [vast] intelligence were moving about undisturbed by my presence." He becomes "convinced that somebody was breathing for both me and himself." With their magical skill, the elders have catapulted Malidoma into the essential Light that is God that is Love that is the Universe—to borrow Lucille's apt formula—the purpose being, in the words of the officiating elder, "to remember where you have come from" so as to be able to "fulfill your duties on this Earth."

Touching Ancestors and the Astral World

Given the biological and psychic links—whether painful or joyous—that connect mothers and daughters, most women are probably not surprised that Lucille's entrée into direct knowledge of the divine world of light should come through her deceased mother. I myself have long felt that death would not sever my relationship with my mother. In fact, I do not want it to. At an earlier point in my life, when I could not imagine being in a world in which my mother did not exist, when her absence would have left a hole too big for me to swallow, the only way I could even begin to accept the dreaded possibility of her leaving me through death was to say to myself that she would come to see me after she physically departed this world. I write this statement now and smilingly acknowledge the unhealed wounding of abandonment it contains. And, even though I no longer need my mother from these depths of deprivation, and, beyond this, possess an informed comfort in the life of the spirit, which somewhat diminishes my previous view of the power or permanence of physical death, I still like knowing that we probably could, if necessary, communicate with one another.

Enduring ties with ancestors was a topic that Dolores Kendrick, another teacher and poet, spoke about confidently. Dolores believes that countless African American forebears—mothers, fathers, and grandparents—have had spiritual connections that sustained them, connections that could be heard sometimes in their language and the way they spoke, connections that they passed on to us, their children. Her own mother often remarked that "God doesn't put anything on you that you can't handle," and Dolores had to remember this when her mother died in

February of 1976. Leaving her mother's funeral, she returned to the apartment that she had occupied with her mother—despite the concern of friends and family who worried about her being there alone.

In the apartment Dolores had kept a small calendar with "wonderful little sayings usually attending to our spiritual natures," which was opened to the week her mother died with its exhortations to, "Remember the lilies of the field." One morning some days later Dolores rose to discover the same phrase scrawled on the calendar in her mother's print. It was rare even in life to see her print; her beautiful cursive was what she regularly used. Dolores recalled coming across this printing of her mother:

> I thought how did that get there? She wasn't even here when that calendar was on my desk. And I never knew or understood how it got there. I ran looking for her occasional print in her own papers and I found it and compared them and surely it was her print. I have that framed and in my room right now. That for me was scary. I just don't know how that happened. But I don't question these things.

Perhaps, as she was crossing over, Dolores's mother wanted to leave her daughter a final word of solace and advice.

Sonia Sanchez, whose creative writing often employs feminine and maternal images, similarly experienced an even more crucial form of contact with her dead mother. Exhausted after giving natural birth to twin sons, Sonia was wheeled into her room and went right to sleep. When she heard someone calling her name, she pulled herself up, despite all the intravenous hookups, and answered, "Yes, yes." A nurse who was passing by heard her, rushed over, and said, "You'd better stretch out. You're already causing enough trouble having two babies in here." Sonia answered, "Someone's calling me," and the nurse replied, "Dear, no one's calling you."

At this point, the nurse began rearranging Sonia's gown and putting her back under the covers, when she noticed her IVs and gasped, "Oh my God." Someone had hooked up her intravenous drips so incorrectly that her stomach had become hard as a rock. The nurse told Sonia to go to sleep. Tired beyond measure and soothed by the reassuring voice, she stretched out and went back down. Had the nurse not corrected the IVs and rubbed her the whole night, she would have died. Next morning the doctor came in and told her, "We almost lost you there last night." Sonia explains the incident by saying, "That was my mother. That was *definitely* my mother. One day I realized my mother had been calling to me, 'Wake up, Sonia, wake up. I died giving birth to twins. You cannot die giving birth to twins. We've got to have progress beyond this.'" Although Sonia knew of her mother's fate, this dramatic contact with her reiterated the generational echoes as well as Sonia's own personal dedication to racial progress.

Similar to Lucille Clifton's recollections of her relationship with her Thelma-Greta, the above stories of Dolores Kendrick and Sonia Sanchez illustrate the strong connections that many women often have with their deceased mothers. Beyond-the-grave contacts that occur in times of grief, need, or danger traditionally have been reported by all kinds of people, and they represent the easiest, most basic line of communication between what we think of as living human beings and what Lucille has termed "the energy that is those who have left their flesh."

These connections made between African American women and the spirits of their mothers are a reminder that being conversant with the spirit world is an aspect of everybody's ancient wisdom. They also suggest that looking close to home for expressions of spirituality may result in an expanded awareness of the aspects of the universe with which we can be in loving and helpful union.

In her personal experience, Namonyah has taken this a step further through her adherence to, in her words, "African-based religions which require the veneration of eguns [ancestors]." Luisah Teish, Yoruba priestess and author of *Jambalaya*, defines egun or *egungun* (from the Yoruba) as "those souls or intelligences who have moved beyond the physical body." "Existing at another level within the creative energy," they are treated with loving reverence—honorably buried, offered food, sung to and danced to, made the focus of theater, and so on. In exchange, they can provide "protection, wisdom, and assistance to those who revere them."

Her relationship with her eguns has enabled Namonyah to open and look through "the crack of the two worlds." Not only does she no longer fear death, but the intellectual knowledge she possessed about the endurance of energy in multiple forms has now become direct, incontrovertible understanding: "I have a sense of what that other world feels like through my ancestors and through going into trance states. It is an actuality." Because of an early and traumatic near-death incident, she says she had lived much of her life "in fear of death." Drawing on Tibetan Buddhist, Native American, Yoruba, and other spiritual teachings helped her to become more aware and less afraid, and to connect with divine energy.

As our conversation ventured deeper and deeper into the subject, Namonyah was hard pressed to talk about these matters. Following is a portion of our discussion:

Namonyah: Let me try to explain it to you, because this is where it gets really difficult, trying to put it into words. The best way that I can try to explain the feeling is to say that it's an energy, but it's an energy that has a sound to it. There's an actual sound and a communication in the energy that vibrates in my body. When I say vibrates, I'm talking about a vibration that happens so much that it separates the subtle body energy from the concrete body energy. I'm saying it's a vibration, but it may even be a light.

Akasha: But you experience it as movement and sound?

Namonyah: I feel it and I hear it and I can see it, but not with these eyes. It's not something that I started out doing consciously, because I was afraid. A whole part of my religious upbringing was watching people in church get happy, and that scared me—to have the Holy Ghost come in. So it's not something that I was seeking, in that way. It's something that happened because I'm on a path, and the more I open up, the more I'm going to be led, and I realized that. Sometimes it would happen with me being in the bed, just in between the moment of sleep, like a twilight experience. And this has been happening to me for years. People call that astral projection. But what is happening to me now is not astral projection, not the way I experience it. It is not outside of me, but a journeying inward. What is happening to me now is that when I become afraid of it, I will actually say, "Aunt Belle," who is one of the eguns, "hold my hand"—and I feel and know that she is holding my hand. And while she's holding my hand, I am saying to myself, "This is incredible, I can't believe that this is happening." But at the same time, I'm feeling it happen. It's not a fantasy or something that I'm reading about or being told about.

Namonyah's remarks show how her experiences parallel Lucille's —how neither sought out supernatural phenomena; how unmistakable such contact was when it came; how they both sensed the "unseen" world as light, sound, and vibration; and how specific was the identity of those they encountered there. Further, just as Lucille's children came to know Thelma-Greta, their dead grandmother, Namonyah's housemates have felt the presence of her eguns. On one occasion, one of her roommates talked off and on for two hours to movement around the house that she thought was Namonyah, who, in fact, was not even at home. Another roommate was frightened by seeing the eguns. Everybody in the house learned that her ancestors were actively present. When I suggested that all of this sounded as if the ancestors were more in her world than she in theirs, Namonyah countered, "But I'm also being pulled into their world." She explains this further:

> When I say to my father, "Hold me," he holds me. And once I'm being held, my body as a physicalness is not like that anymore. . . . That reality for me changes. . . . It's like that tingling, that energy . . . That's them [the eguns, ancestors] in terms of how they manifest themselves. There's no separation. It's different from me watching a shadow around my altar or a candle go out

or a candle flip. When I say directly, "Contact me," that energy merges with me, and my body ceases to be my body as I was experiencing it prior to that energy merging with mine. Then all that I am experiencing is an energy that is alive, that communicates, and that makes me laugh because I feel God, because I feel that there's no difference. It's like there's a knowing that takes place and then the laughter comes because in that moment I understand everything. . . . It may take ten years to write about it, but in that moment, it's phenomenal.

What Namonyah describes here is the transcendent spiritual experience of blissful oneness that other seekers have likewise groped to encapsulate in words. However, she is astute in her understanding that "this is a portion of it [divine unity] as it relates to my eguns being a part of it and being . . . it's so hard to articulate this stuff. They're a part of it, but at the same time they're like the direct stepping stones to that total transcendence." She goes on to concur that touching them puts her in touch with it "in that the distance between Heaven and Earth is shortened." This piece of my conversation with Namonyah changed forever my attitude toward ancestor reverence, which I had eschewed in favor of less personalized, more unmediated and "purer" avenues of access to the divine.

It helped me to appreciate that those who have loved us, who have been released into the state of greater awareness that we mistakenly and totalizingly call "death," can help induct us into expanded and divine consciousness. And though this point of entry—while contiguous with and inseparable from the all—does not represent the highest realms or energies, used with spiritual understanding and integrity such as Namonyah brings to it, it is a very valuable doorway to what she called "that total transcendence." Of course, this recognition of the divine role of the ancestors accords perfectly with traditional African philosophy.

Ancestral presences typically inhabit the astral plane, which is experienced by many people through occasional forays into that dimension that are usually remembered as a nighttime dream of flying. Beyond this common experience, it appears that humankind is generally becoming more aware of the astral dimension and is moving toward being able to function with consciousness and control on (or in) it. It is interesting that Lucille notes how her mother, Thelma, is "quite like she always was," getting enjoyment from finding parking spaces for people who ask her for them because she herself never learned to drive. Because the astral level is the next major layer beyond the physical, it makes sense that much of what individuals carry in the physical body on Earth does not immediately drop after death. I have read stories about newly dead souls who come through to awareness on this astral plane and do not realize right away that any change has even occurred.

The affirmation that ancestors reside all around us, that, to use Lucille's words, "they are present as air" has been popularized through African poet Birago Diop's poem, "Breaths," which the black women's musical group Sweet Honey in the Rock adapted and then recorded for their album "Good News." The lyrics of this song run, in part:

> Those who have died have never never left
> The dead have a pact with the living
> They are in the woman's breast

They are in the wailing child
They are with us in the home
They are with us in the crowd
The dead have a pact with the living

About this fact of spiritual continuation after physical death, Dolores's initial reaction was fear and bafflement when she confirmed that her departing mother had indeed left her a handprinted note. Now, as she remarked during our conversations, she "doesn't question these things." This stance echoes the open-minded, open-ended attitude taken by many who have experienced similar happenings or believe in their possibility. This willingness to suspend disbelief signals a kind of acceptance—even if it also implies that spiritual reality will not be scrutinized too closely or pondered too deeply. Perhaps the countless generations before us who have lived in conscious communication with the spirit world make it somewhat easier for African American women like Dolores "not to question." Certainly, too, we have heard the spirits sing along with us in southern churches and march beside us on threatening Alabama streets. Now, in this momentous New Age, attitudes of nonjudgmental acceptance of supernatural phenomena are becoming increasingly common. And black women's openness about their own experiences with spirit contact is a major contributing factor.

In general, as compared to the past, today there is a stronger inclination to talk about personal contacts from "beyond the veil," more knowledgeable instances of and discussion about astral projection, and greater disclosure by creative artists about the channeling of their characters from beings on this other-worldly plane (a subject I take up in chapter 4). It is because of this increased discourse that Toni Morrison can write a world-class novel such as *Beloved* based on a ghostly reappearance and have that premise accepted by millions of readers who do not require literary explanations of magical realism or the one-dimensional presentation of the ghost-character as only a figment of the imagination.

As human beings continue to become more astrally proficient, they demonstrate an advance in the abilities of our evolving species. However, many spiritual traditions and teachers say that care should be taken in this regard. Different religious and metaphysical systems have their own particular ways of referring to the subtle dimensions surrounding the physical body, but in theosophical considerations, the term "astral" is used and the subject is given significant attention. For one thing, the astral body and the general plane of which it is a part is said to be the realm of desire and emotional energy. This emotional energy, as most people presently use it, is extremely charged and powerful, whether for good or ill. When used for good, it is wonderful—a requisite force for getting things done, making anything manifest, cooperating with creation. When used for ill, it can be disastrous.

In short, the astral world is a complicated place and each person living is busy working there because we all have desires and emotions. The "potency of human desire and of world desire" produces a constant pouring forth of our pictures of what we desire, images that are concretized in astral matter. One place where this process is explained is the esoteric text, *A Treatise on White Magic*, which was transcribed by Alice Bailey in 1934 from a teacher on the spiritual plane. The description of the astral world given in this work is helpful, I think, for the way it succinctly pulls together information about the nature of emotions and desire, the beings of the astral plane, and the "concrete" manifestations that are temporarily built out of etheric, akashic matter:

> Individual desire, national desire, racial desire, the desire of humanity as a whole, plus the instinctual desire of all subhuman lives causes a constant changing and shifting of the substance of the plane; there is a building of the temporary forms, some of rare beauty, some of no beauty, and a vitalizing by the astral energy of its creator. Add to these forms that persistent and steadily growing scenario we call the "akashic records" which concern the emotional history of the past, add the activities of the discarnate lives which are passing through the astral plane, either out of or towards incarnation, add the potent desire, purified and intelligent, of all superhuman Lives . . . and the sum total of forces present is stupendous.

Given the theory that everything is energetically connected, then all of these forces course around and through each one of us, and we respond to them according to our overall makeup. Because the astral world teems with highly desirable as well as very undesirable entities and energy, careless trafficking in it, unqualified glee about any possible activity on it, or psychic joyriding around it is probably ill-advised. Further, becoming astrally proficient would mean we would learn to practice discrimination—separating out which part of the astral mix is who we are, determining what parts are positive, and so on—and detachment—remaining in control of ourselves, and free of whatever we decide is not right for us. As we have seen with earlier examples, African American women are clearly available for contact with the astral world. Consciously or unconsciously, the experiences we absorb from our culture regarding that world help to instill respect and carefulness about it. Lucille, Dolores, Sonia, and Namonyah had no horror stories to report. This may be because they did not go out of their way to make the contacts; benevolent beings and energies sought them out.

Finally, by possessing greater experience and understanding of the astral world, individuals may eventually harbor less fear of death, which, at present, is one of the largest "blockers of energy," to borrow Lucille's phrase. Perhaps some of the terrors of death could be dispelled by simply spending time with the beings and energy from this place that people first inhabit when they relinquish life in the physical dimension. We might then come to know that the energy that is essentially ourselves, our spiritual consciousness, does not cease to exist—as Sweet Honey sings, "those who have died have never never left," and as Lucille says, "energy doesn't dissolve." We could then possibly entertain the thought that life on Earth is only one phase of a many-layered continuum of being. With that knowledge we could more easily untie our attachment to fulfillment of the self, detach from the solely corporeal perspective, and discover Namonyah's bliss of light that awaits us on more transcendent levels. Overall, the testimonies of African American women encourage our envisioning of an Aquarian time when expansive, spiritual connection will characterize the whole of human society and help to make this world a better place to live, on every level.

ᴈᴈᴈ 3 ᴈᴈᴈ

RACE, RACISM, AND SPIRITUALITY:
Uniting Politics and Spirit Day by Day

When the women I associated with began using the word "spiritual" in the late 1970s, we never paused to say exactly what we meant or what precisely we were talking about. Clearly, it was a shorthand way of referring to the divine grace and support both beyond and within ourselves that enabled us to survive as marginalized black women. Many of us were breaking with traditional, Western, Christian-based religions and adopting generically New Age practices that included such modalities as natural altars, Tarot readings, meditation, and metaphysics. Yet, this new spirituality we fashioned is still very much a black women's "thing," because it is, by definition, a black female creation and because of its incorporation of African-derived consciousness and elements.

More important, still, is the fact that any definition or

conceptualization of spirituality among African American women eventually veers into and takes into account racial oppression and other socio-political conditions. That spirituality should be a tool for combating racism and injustice is a foundational and prevailing idea. Acts of hatred that have bombarded black women personally and collectively have forced us toward this type of socially grounded and socially contextualized definition. We are nevertheless able to affirm grandly the unifying rightness and power of transcendent love. Just as we wear our politicized identities every hour of every day, we lean toward spiritual practices that are concrete and can easily be incorporated into daily life. Overall, African- American women articulate a spirituality that is, on the one hand, deep, esoteric, and universal and, on the other, anchored in the body and the material world, as well as race- and gender-specific in its assumptions and applications.

I begin this chapter with four wonderful stories that illustrate this very important fundamental point.

Defining Spirituality: Several Stories Charged with Political Implications

Story 1: A Conversation with Alice Walker

I began speaking with Alice Walker about spirituality and, almost immediately, we were at loggerheads. Alice said she "took issue" with the notion of the "supernatural." She emphatically declared that "everything is natural" and proceeded to amplify her position:

> All of it is natural. I mean, speaking to spirits, whoever is around you, whoever is inside you, it's perfectly natural; there's nothing supernatural about it. I mean, we're

here on the Earth, we're on the planet. They're here on the Earth, they're on the planet. Nobody has ever gone anywhere. That's why they're still here.

She made a few more observations to this effect, after which I intervened with what I thought was a sensible, ameliorative statement about the word "supernatural" being just a convenient way we had of referring to a reality "that we do not usually consciously tune into or avow." And, yes, I continued, it was as the spiritual and esoteric folk said: The real world is a world that you don't see, and this one is essentially phenomena and illusion. She quickly interjected, "Well, see, I disagree with that," and she explained that "the real world is all of it, obviously. It's what you see and what you don't see. How could it be otherwise? And what point is there in trying to live for something that you don't know, that you think is not there?" I replied that, of course, this phenomenal world we live in is real in the sense that it is where we work out who we are and so forth, but as our forebears used to say, this is not my home. Alice, again, laughingly replied: "However, you see, I also take a little bit of issue with the forebears! I take issue with all of it!"

Not wanting to get bogged down in semantics, and in order for us to move on, I gave up—and reminded her that Barbara Christian, the black feminist critic who has written extensively about her work, said that what defined her, Alice Walker, was her contrariness. Still nonplussed, she got in the last word to this "contrary" exchange between us:

This is my home. I'm here, and this is my home. And that's why I'm here. If there is a home somewhere else for me, I will probably get there. But actually, I'm not concerned because I'm happy here. I'm an earthling, I was born here, I know the place. I have no desire really to travel. I don't want to go to the moon, I don't want to go to the stars. Venus can be happy without my presence. So I think what they [the forebears] really meant was more a condition, I mean a condition of servitude and oppression, and that is *not* your home. Oppression is not your home, and people should stop being so comfortable in it.

Story 2: Speaking with Masani Alexis DeVeaux

After almost two hours of enjoyable rapport between us, Masani Alexis DeVeaux wound up an impassioned statement about the transformative changes she sees occurring all around us by saying, "I think that we're in an era where more and more—I can't say most—but more and more people are conscious about what they have to do."

"On the spiritual level?" I queried.

"Spiritual, political, social, and emotional levels," was her response, and she proceeded to give examples of change taking place at the level of black women who do not have ample economic resources but who have children in schools and go to those schools when their kids are being miseducated. Taking on the voices of those women, she lined it out:

> "My daughter don't know nuttin' about black history. How come you're not teaching it?" Change is taking place at that level. Or "I'm tired of you telling me that my child is slow. My child is not slow. You don't know how to teach. Have you ever thought of that? You don't know

how to teach, because if you knew how to teach, you would be able to distinguish the different skills of different students, and you would make the child who appears to you to have fewer skills as important as the child who appears to be brilliant." And the mother who says, "I'm tired of you telling me that my child cannot learn," is being as active as any of us who are teaching at the college level or writing big books or whatever. So I think it's everywhere, and it's at the level where people are at. And that's what has to be recognized.

When I questioned whether that kind of activity could, technically speaking, be termed spiritual, Masani Alexis called on me to rethink a possibly limiting conception of spirituality: "Those mothers might be channeling in a way that you haven't thought of. And so that challenges you to open up and broaden your sense of what you think is channeling and what you think is spiritual." In short, she unequivocally rejected any idea of spirituality that did not include the sister who is giving the public school system justified hell.

Story 3: Travels with Namonyah Soipan

Namonyah Soipan and I had a very intense exchange toward the end of my interview with her. She was explaining to me her understanding of the relationship between reality, symbols, and the spiritual realm. Seeing my chance, I asked: "So, working analogously on that same principle is why you want to carry your ancestors around in your trunk?" (She and I were on vacation together in Ghana, sharing time and each other's baggage, so to speak.) Her answer was "no." Her ancestors were present without their urn. That being so, I persisted, there was still apparently something that compelled her to have the actual urn:

Namonyah: Suppose God decided to keep all this incredible beauty we're looking at within Him- and Herself. The whole reason for creation is that God wanted to behold God. Everything that is created now is because God wanted to behold his or her own divine essence. Suppose God decided, I don't want to behold myself, I can just be. We wouldn't have any of this. So, yes, I want to behold my own divine essence. But I don't need a shrine, I don't have to sit there. I can meditate anywhere.

Akasha: Yes, so why is that important?

Namonyah: Because I'm beholding me. For me to sit at my shrine and feel that vortex of energy there that I've created through my own divine essence and know that it's still there, that's me beholding me. It's almost like a reflection.

Akasha: But why do you have to do it concretely when you can do it on the plane of mind? When you know it is you without being materialized?

Namonyah: Because I'm concrete and material as well as spiritual. There's an aspect of me that's concrete and material, so why can't I have an aspect of the divine that is concrete and material, just like there's an aspect of me that is spiritual?

We went on in this heated way for some minutes more. The breeze off the ocean at Coco Beach, Accra, was a very good thing.

Namonyah let me know that I could use the word "symbolic" instead of the words "material" or "concrete": "When white men penetrated African spirituality and thought they [the Africans] were worshipping idols, they didn't understand the whole sophisticated system of symbolism and how it healed and how it worked on the spiritual plane. They didn't see it. They only saw the Africans sitting here looking at that cow or that ankh or that third eye or that stone."

At this point, I stopped pressing Namonyah to explain. I understood what she was saying and the correlations that were being made. Just as the manifested, physical universe is a symbol of God the divine, so her ancestral urn carries the symbolic manifestation of the spiritual energy that is her eguns. So, too, does she meet her own spiritual self in the vortex of energy that she has created by persistently sitting her physical self before her shrine. Everything in existence exists at multiple levels, from the concrete and material to the spiritual. Not to understand this relationship between the seen and the unseen is spiritual ignorance tantamount to that exhibited by the white men who came to Africa and violated its deep and complex spirituality.

Story 4: An Exchange with Toni Cade Bambara

After a long interview in which we had talked about spirituality in many of its various personal, cultural, literary, and social forms, Toni Cade Bambara and I realized the recording machine had come to the last bit of tape. To conclude, I asked her if there was "anything final she'd like to say about herself as a spiritual being and the manifestation of that" in her work. Her answer totally shocked me:

Toni: No. *Spiritual being* bothers me. I'm not a spiritual being.

Akasha: [in surprise] You're not?

Toni: No. And I'm trying to figure out why not. Spiritual being. A lot of people I can think of—I'd call them spiritual beings. I don't think of myself as a spiritual being . . . .

Akasha: A being who operates spiritually. [both a statement and a question]

Toni: Well, I mostly operate on the mundane level, though. If mind-body-spirit was one word—which I'm trying to make one word in my life—it would be wonderful if we could be that kind of mind-body-spirit, without the slash, without the hyphen, and without the space between, and without the "and/or."

Akasha: We'll have to translate first here [translate means "die"], and then we would be it. No, then we would have dropped out all the other stuff, and there would be just spirit.

Toni: I don't think so. That's not where I'm going. I'm going mind-body-spirit one word. I'm heading there, and so that's one of the reasons I sort of frown when you say spiritual being. I'm not a spiritual being. I'm very much grounded and mundane and political and historical. But I also know where I live, what fuels that work.

Akasha: And that . . . ?

Toni: Something else.

Akasha: This something else that we keep not having the name for?

Toni: Some people call it spirit, spiritual, which I do, too. I say some people, also me! But I'm looking for another word for it. I'm looking for something else, because when I throw that word, put that word on top of it, whatever that is that's squishing, there's a whole lot of other stuff still squishing out there that's not covered with that word.

Akasha: What else is squishing out?

Toni: I mean, doesn't cover it. It's not adequate. It might feel accurate, but it's not adequate, doesn't cover it.

Akasha: And there is no word, or even words to even try to get that?

Toni: Not that I know of. I mean, not that I know of in English. There might very well be, but I don't know. No, I'm leaning for mind-body-spirit. Which is no small feat.

※

Each of the women in these conversations took pains to define her spirituality in racial and social terms. During our exchange about what was "supernatural," Alice denounced "servitude and oppression." Masani Alexis refused to divorce the spiritual from the "political, social, and emotional." Namonyah implicitly equated white racist arrogance with spiritual obtuseness. Toni insisted upon her "mundane and political and historical" identity. Because of the realities of our lives, African American women are compelled to conceptualize and practice spirituality in ways that others, especially white men and women, may not have to. Many people talk about their spirituality and never indicate any awareness that it is socially embedded or could be used in a socially responsive way to fight societal ills. This is rarely the case with black women.

When I spoke with Sonia Sanchez, for example, she took the idea of spirituality even more forcefully into racial and political arenas by making three essential observations. The first is that African American spirituality has always powered our racial activism. It has been the "moral core" that built schools, colleges, and churches, and it has been the account African Americans have drawn from to "maintain our trust in this land, this earth." That spirit, Sonia Sanchez asserts, is what we are invoking when we look at old photographs and family scrapbooks: "Well, this one right here was the drunk of the family. This one here was the one who spit in the bus driver's face." Among our varied kin, we can always find some one or another whose spiritual and spirited sense of self led to acts—whether large or small—of resistance to oppression.

The second important point Sonia made is that this kind of spiritual consciousness challenges the materialism that pervades Western thinking and, consequently, it is always being suppressed by the entrenched status quo: "If you really begin to teach people not just to compete all the time, but also to just let people be and move in a gentle, kind way towards each other, then, in no uncertain terms, you would have a different kind of people on this Earth. You would not have the kind of people who would be willing to chop off heads to acquire stuff. You wouldn't have the materialistic place that we have now." The forces who run the world want to "keep us relegated to the lowest level," Sonia says, "grinding, eating, always stuffing ourselves, getting overstuffed on sex, with anything, whatever." Then it becomes difficult to rise above that and think a higher thought. A society of people "who can really see and have vision" cannot be controlled.

Finally, Sonia took to task those who possess spiritual information and knowledge but use it only for their own selfish ends, wallowing in self-aggrandizement. Listening to such people hold forth about what they know, she thinks of asking them, "Well, have you ever explained that to people? Do you take that out to people?" She believes that everyone is capable of learning—anything. Like the priests of ancient Egypt who hoarded their spiritual wisdom and kept the masses ignorant, thereby leaving the culture vulnerable for conquering, members of certain African American spiritual communities today, who regard what they know as privileged and secret, are hoarding their spiritual knowledge, which is ultimately a self-destructive act. They can feel superior and revel in their power, "but you see, my sister," says Sonia, "power to me, the point of having power, of knowing something is to also empower other people." Overall, Sonia regards spirituality—as do many other African American women—as yet another tool for unified consciousness and action, a means to make the world a better place for all of us to live.

In the same way that education and betterment of the African American race traditionally have been cornerstones of black culture, the spiritual vision of African American women also includes study and personal striving toward improvement. At the point in our interview where Sonia and I spoke about teaching ancient wisdom to all people, she distinguished between "natural" and "learned" spirituality. Yet even those who possess extraordinary abilities such as clairvoyance or a strong in-tuition can still "learn" spirituality in the sense that study and application can hone and further develop what is innately spiri-tual in them.

When I asked Toni Cade Bambara to talk about what she has done to sharpen her spiritual knowledge, she gave three ex-amples: she reads widely in books that call themselves to her attention (as when she walks into a candle or herb shop and picks up the dirty, stepped-on, ripped-up, falling-apart book she finds lying on the floor and waiting just for her); she seeks out "light-bearing" groups in new communities (for instance, she'll go into a print shop in a black neighborhood and look at their bulletin board or ask them if they have done any flyers lately for any "healing and light" type of group); and she'll allow herself to be led to teachers through an attunement to the meaning of given names, as she explains it:

> When I was in Atlanta, I heard of a clairvoyant named Vera. My ears always perk up for somebody with that name, *truth*. Or a name like Lucille, *light*. One of my best friends was named Luce and my other friend was Clare. But, anyway, I got very interested in her [Vera]. A lot of my friends were taking workshops with her. She was a nurse, and she had the ability to do internal-medical health readings over the phone. She was pre-cognate, she can give you precognitive readings. I knew a lot of people who were taking workshops with her in effective prayer—which I'm not interested in. She also ran a dream workshop and some other different workshops. So I went to study under her. What did I study? It was a dream workshop, and it was terribly helpful at that time. In

other words, I was able to make use of dream life to get some work done.

A later and *lighter* exchange about developing supernormal abilities ensued when Toni turned the proverbial tables on our interview and asked me what I had done for the recent spring equinox. In answering her question, I began describing a trip to the ocean at night with friends when Toni interrupted with an affirmation of that activity as "the conscious reconstruction of the ritual life—yeah, yeah, good." Then, we segued into a long discussion of the various kinds of spiritual teaching that are available. Her enthusiastic report about one black woman's workshop produced the following funny dialogue:

Toni: Sometimes she might give a workshop called "Spirit in the Something," and you will learn how to meditate or levitate. I'm not sure what she teaches in that, but basically you're working on yourself.

Akasha: You're kind of joking when you say levitate.

Toni: No, I know many people who can levitate, and so do you. You know ———. I think you met her. She's a dean now at ———. She can levitate. A lot of people can levitate. It's only air.

Akasha: Yes. Can you levitate?

Toni: No, doesn't interest me. Does it interest you?

Akasha: No.

Toni: Because I could send you to somebody.

Akasha: No, there are other things I want to do first.

"Right," Toni said, and then she recalled the time she passed up—with due respect—studying rainmaking under a Cree medicine teacher. I am not sure what I would have answered if, instead of proceeding to tell her Cree rainmaking story, Toni had asked me what were the other things that I wanted to learn. This lifetime for me is not one characterized by phenomenal spiritual abilities. I believe that other lifetimes have been, but not this one. My earlier tendency to yearn for what I no longer possess has been greatly mitigated by an understanding that psychic sensitivity does not necessarily mean spiritual evolvement. My main point here, however, is that this exchange between Toni and me underscores the fact that many contemporary African American women take spiritual development seriously, understanding it as one more tool in the arsenal we use to help ourselves and the wider world.

Spiritual Visions and Visionaries

Despite their need to do political battle, black women can be full of a sense of spirituality that is transcendent. Geraldine McIntosh, for example, is a human resources specialist who must often rail against the both subtle and egregious breaches of affirmative rights that she encounters in her work. Yet when I spoke with her, she launched without prelude or preamble into a deep and beautiful formulation of what spirituality is to her:

> I think about it in terms of being connected, and I think that that connection happens because of something intrinsic and is not maintained by extrinsic things. . . . And that's the "nth" of my spirituality, like the height or the depth of it, the very core of what my spirituality is. And

I started talking about it this way after I read Octavia Butler.

The specific books by black female science fiction and fantasy writer Octavia E. Butler to which Geraldine referred were *Wild Seed* (1980), *Mind of My Mind* (1977), and *Patternmaster* (1976). Their publication during these years highlights—once again—the stepped-up creative and evolutionary spiritual activity surrounding 1980, and it further demonstrates the fact that a community of African American women touched by New Age energies were influencing each other, and the world.

For Geraldine, Octavia E. Butler's work was the place where she saw, symbolically reflected, her sense of spirituality as intrinsic connection. To pull this out as a key aspect of Butler's novels is most striking because Butler, like Geraldine herself, views connection—and sometimes even love—as a force that can operate beyond, in spite of, and enmeshed with very grungy stuff like violence, deceit, and greed. Geraldine explained, touching her heart, that spiritual connection feels centered there and is not interrupted by any earthly things. "It feels like there's something inside of me that really is out in the cosmos somewhere, that is a wholeness, and when I got to a certain place, I connected to it." We continued:

> *Geraldine:* I think somehow, all of my life, I've been connected to this universal spirit out there that everything else is connected to, and it's the thing that leads you to your next opportunity, that pushes you into the next growth you need. That felt out of control, so I worked on learning how to name it, how to call it.
>
> *Akasha:* What did you name it?

Geraldine: I named it Spirit. I named it Connection. I named it all this conversation that I'm having with you because, before, people would say, "That's a haphazard goddamn kind of life to have." But it led me to the right thing, even when I went wrong.

Akasha: So, do you think there is any advantage, or any increase in anything, or any benefit to naming it and then being consciously aware that there is such a force and a mechanism happening?

Geraldine: It's only a benefit to name it when you live in a capitalistic system where the people are wanting one up and one down. I think if it were not for that system there would be no benefit in naming it, because you do not have to have language to pass it on. People know. I can walk down the hall and look at people and they say I'm warm when I'm being nasty. People know. This is something that just radiates. Somehow, even when people are all bound with shit, they can still look at my smile. . . .

Akasha: And what do they see?

Geraldine: They see caring. They see all that kind of intrinsic soul stuff about me, even when I'm pissed, even when I don't like white people, the white people that I don't like will say, "Oh, she's so sensitive." They say I'm caring, sensitive, all that stuff about I know how to do people. What that is, is sameness with all people. One of the reasons why I had to name it is no one gave me value for owning this. I never got credit for having it until I could name it, talk about it in the way that they're writing about it today.

Akasha: Okay, so these people who just run into you as you walk the halls at work, what's coming out to them is this automatic connection, caring thing. . . .

Geraldine: They may not talk about what they're registering in terms of caring. They will talk about it in terms of wherever it is they're open. . . . They know they don't have to put up a barrier because *I ain't got one up.* See, I think people can sense that. That's what the spirit is about. . . . That's how I think it plays itself out in my everyday life.

Akasha: Well, then, that would totally be your everyday life because it's about how you just walk around in the world, it's about every encounter you have with every other living being.

Geraldine: It happens with cats and dogs, too.

In this exchange, Geraldine characterizes the "universal spirit" to which everything is connected using a number of key phrases and concepts—as a directing energy that pushes sequential growth; as beyond the comfort needs of the little, rational mind; as totally communicable but not dependent on language for its communication; as radiated warmth and caring and openness that can override and penetrate personality blockages; as a fundamental sameness and identification with all living things. It seems accurate that her shorthand for all these qualities is "all that kind of intrinsic soul stuff," for they are the characteristics that people who believe in the soul usually attribute to it. This concept of the soul starts with the idea that, on the physical level, everything that exists is united in etheric substance (the intangible—from a gross point of view—building-blocks material of the universe), and that, through this etheric substance, spirit acts and produces soul consciousness. Thus, all of life is holographically connected; there is no "here" or "there," no "self" and "other."

As such, the essence of this "soul stuff" would be love—not the simple-minded sentiment that love so often becomes in the hands of us evolving-but-not-there-yet human beings, but the powerful energy that gave rise to and continues to sustain all that exists—what Dylan Thomas refers to as "the force that through the green fuse drives the flower," in his poem titled after this line; what Lucille Clifton knows when she encapsulates in an extemporaneous remark that "you are not your brother's keeper, you are your brother." In conscious practice, this love would become what M. Scott Peck defines as "the will to extend one's self for the purpose of nurturing one's own or another's growth"—an inclusiveness, understanding, and empathy that radiates, magnetizes, actualizes whatever can be benefited by it.

Alice Walker's spiritual vision is likewise based on and empowered by an expansive kind of love. When I asked her about her spiritual gifts, she responded in this way:

Alice: My only spiritual gift is love, and I think that out of that love I can heal—heal myself and somebody or something else. . . . But, you know, I don't think of it as healing, I just think of it as loving. That's what love does. And it's just the way to be in the world.

Akasha: How did you come to understand love in the profound way that you do now?

Alice: At some point I kind of got it. When I was initiated as a meditator, I had gone through the whole training and everything . . . and when I finally got it, I started to laugh. And I haven't stopped laughing because what you get, what you understand, is that you are loved. It doesn't have to be by Joe Blow and Jane P. or whoever. It doesn't have to be *by* anyone. You are loved, just you, as you are. And how can you walk out in the sunshine and feel the wind in your hair and put your feet on the grass and not know that?

Akasha: And then it was easy just to bring your life in line with that, to just live it?

Alice: I don't know about how easy because sometimes people make you want to kill them—although I haven't felt that way in a while. But I still sometimes feel very rageful about what is happening to people and to the Earth. I'm just human. But overall, I can just feel it. In a way, it *is* inexplicable—how you just meet people and you love them. I mean, you may never see them again, but you just love them because they are.

Akasha: So, somehow or another, you have managed to really get to a place in yourself of knowing that you are not separate from other people?

Alice: No, I'm not. . . .

Akasha: And being able to make that a living reality?

Alice: Not even from chickens and pigs and turkeys.

Akasha: Yes. So that first knowing came through meditation. . . .

Alice: You know, it didn't come first through meditation. That was what I understood after I learned meditation. What meditation took me back to was the way I was as a child, and that's why I think people, children come into the world as loving beings, knowing they are loved. That's the paradise that's lost, that feeling of being at one with everyone and everything.

When they speak about connectedness and about "being at one with everyone and everything," Geraldine and Alice pull us into the very heart of spiritual consciousness, to a center where spirituality reposes as the universal, loving connection to all living things, and as a natural, unconditional, and healing love. This idea is based on the usually unarticulated knowledge that, despite all differences and appearances to the contrary, there is an order larger than this visible one that holds everything together. Because it is normally not stated and because it makes space for both "religious" and "scientific" paths to the divine, this is the root, the defining reality of spirituality that I always try to emphasize.

It is a consciousness where external factors that usually make for difference and separateness cease to be considerations—whether they are factors of race, age, gender, or even species, an observation that can be made since both Alice and Geraldine quickly and voluntarily state their connection with dogs, cats, chickens, and other animals. Maintaining this all-embracing "oneness" is not always easy for them. Alice mentions her sometimes "rageful" feelings. Geraldine makes obvious her dislike of white people's racism—even as they, ironically, continue to respond to her spiritually generated warmth and persist in liking her.

Although I understand it because I too experience it within myself, it is amazing to me that black women—who have been ostracized and "other'ed," who have had their noses rubbed since birth in segregation and spurious discrimination—are still able to witness for all-inclusive love, non-exclusive unity. This does not mean that we are blind or stupid, for we are acutely observant of all violations of the law of human (and other) connection. It is just that, propelled by the transcendent truth of a deep spirituality, we struggle to choose love and relationship.

Spiritual Wisdom, Everyday Use

In Alice Walker's short story, "Everyday Use," the act of spreading a revered ancestral quilt on the bed to keep warm is more laudable than distantly hanging it on the wall as a nouveau art object. The lesson here is that the spirituality of the quiltmaker expresses itself in a homely and functional object, the purpose of which is best fulfilled when it is freely used and enjoyed in everyday life. Following similar impulses, African American women orient toward useful and daily spiritual practices—those that they weave into their household environment and activities, those that are simple but effective ways of affirming divine connection. What Masani Alexis DeVeaux and Michele Gibbs disclosed about their spiritual routines illustrates this point.

Masani Alexis mentioned the transcendental meditation taught to her by black actor and director Bill Duke as her most "formalized form" of worship. She then enumerated prayer (adding, "I pray a lot"), lighting symbolically appropriate colored candles (such as green when she really needs money), and burning incense as other everyday spiritual acts. But most of what she shared and most of her spiritual practice centers around her two main altars. As she described them, she herself was struck for the first time by the fact that she keeps two of them and that they serve clearly distinct purposes. One of them is in the room where she plays music, a room with many mirrors to reflect her image. Everything about this altar is related to water because Masani Alexis feels connected to the Yoruba ocean goddess Yemanya, whose blue and white waist beads Masani also wears. Here, to this altar, is where she comes to meditate, and where she keeps the affirmations that she repeats every day. The color brown is a very strong presence.

By contrast, "high purples and pinks and some blues"—and also silence—predominate in the bedroom that houses the other altar. Here, there are different kinds of incense. The theme is air or, as Masani Alexis states it, "what's in the air, and changing the air around me because I'm all air. All my signs are air. My sun is Libra, my moon is in Gemini, my rising sign is Aquarius." She needs large drafts of air around her—even if it is cold—in order to breathe. A huge sculpture by Valerie Maynard called "The Oracle," consisting of many faces, looks down upon the surface where the incense burns. On the altar is sand, which Masani Alexis brought back from the pyramids in Egypt. This altar incorporates words. In Masani's handwriting a small sign reads: WHAT THE MIND CAN IMAGINE, THE MIND CAN MANIFEST. Not surprisingly, she does creative visualization in this room. "Yes," says Masani, "that's the room I sit in when I need to draw myself together and be most powerful for whatever situation I have to face. I go in there to be alone, and to reconstruct myself." Masani Alexis sums up her spiritual practice, asserting:

> I do something everyday. Something. Whether it's light a candle, or still myself, or reconstruct myself, or say my affirmations, or thank the universe. But something every day. I think that if I don't, I won't live. And I won't be powerful if I don't, because I also know that that's what's historically kept us alive, that touch with other worlds and other experiences. Or we wouldn't have had stories about people walking on the water back to Africa. So I cannot exist and not pay homage to that. I can't. Otherwise I would stop existing just like that [snaps her fingers]. So that's why I have to do something every day. It's like the first breath is that acknowledgment. I used to be into yoga a lot and tai chi, but right now I'm not. Now it seems to me more about breath and prayer and joining the universe every twenty-four hours.

Interestingly, the great psychologist C. G. Jung (who believed in synchronicity and wrote a foreword for the most-used edition of the ancient Chinese divination method, the I Ching) once said, "Explore daily the will of God."

Michele likewise approached her spirituality in terms of daily ritual, and asserted that she practiced meditation in "a variety of ways." For her, her art work is one form of meditation. It is what she believes she is "here in the world to do." She has always known this, despite being "too busy being socially responsible to do it." She delineated the other elements of her spiritual practice in a wonderfully orderly fashion:

First on her list, after her art, is cooking. Something she began in graduate school as a creative alternative to reading books, cooking is, for Michele, "a meditation in itself." She continues, "Sometimes I think there's nothing more beautiful than browning millet in a pan. I mean, just watching those individual grains, you can take yourself out by looking at the bottom of the pan. So those aspects—texture, color, nutrients, the preparation of nutrients. I never tear or rip or mangle vegetables. Things like that put you in touch, again, with organic reality."

After cooking, Michele lists being with her partner, George. She declares this part of her life to be "crucially crucial . . . healing, expanding, getting in touch with everything." Having this sort of relationship is a spiritual experience, Michele says, because it "dissolves boundaries [between yourself and another person]. It creates another space, another dimension." They touch each other often, but usually "go for hours without a word."

The next action Michele takes toward maintaining her own everyday spiritual practice is committing herself to doing only one other thing per day in addition to the basic activities that are her real life. The "one other thing" could be meeting someone for coffee or lunch, going grocery shopping, returning a book to the library. Limiting these kinds of activities, which can be very sustaining but which often become consuming at the expense of more essential, inner occupations, is a strategy Michele uses to short-circuit old, self-sabotaging habits on a functional level. This extremely valid and helpful tactic is something that I—and I believe many others—could fruitfully adopt.

The one other spiritual act that Michele performs daily is reading the Sacred Path cards. Formally consulting "the universe" as a feature of her spiritual practice is something she does because,

in her exuberant words, "I like it! I like it!" She describes the
Sacred Path cards as "similar to the Tarot, but based on Native
American teachings, primarily having to do with an assessment
of how each person is doing on his or her own spiritual path. It's
not prescriptive. There's no bad news in the cards. There is a
joker, but that's supposed to make you laugh. It's different from
the Tarot in that respect." When we spoke, Michele had been
using them to "check in" daily for about a year, and she also
kept track of her readings. "This method of talking to myself,"
as she phrases it, interested her after a friend had introduced her
to the companion spirit animal deck. Depending on the question she is holding in mind, she does one of the five possible
spreads. Michele explains these:

> The spreads reflect different emphases. For example,
> there's a tepee spread that is an eight-card spread that
> goes up, which is an overall life-path thing. There's the
> four directions spread that has to do with how your male
> and female sides are balanced. There's the kiva spread
> you only do once in your life, so be careful.

The New Year's Eve before our interview, at the end of her
forty-fifth year, Michele had done that kiva spread to mark the
beginning of what she hoped would be "a new cycle." The reading is a ten-card reenactment of a Native American purification
ceremony in which one descends underground and, with the aid
of spirit guides, journeys through to the end having gained the
necessary knowledge to go forward. Pivotal cards are the first,
the fifth, and the tenth:

> The first card, which is the spirit you came here with, was,
> in my case, the storyteller, a card signifying expansion of

consciousness, yours and others, and your mission to do that with other people as well as with yourself. . . . The fifth card is what you need to keep in touch with in order to fulfill your potential. And for me that was also card number five in the whole forty-four-card deck, and it's the standing people, which signifies roots, giving, and your relationship to the Earth. And the tenth card is the at-the-moment card, how you're doing and I got card number twenty, which means victory, advance, you're doing the right thing. My meditation card was rolling rainbow. The rolling rainbow stands for unity and wholeness achieved, particularly across the artificial divisions of the present moment.

In her consulting of these Sacred Path cards, Michele, an African American woman, is drawing on Native American traditions that have been marketed for the New Age in order to help devise a spiritual practice that fulfills the African-based folk criteria of being suitable for "everyday use." Her eclectic, creative approach is representative of the new spirituality of many other black women.

Michele's use of these cards also highlights the fact that readings, reading, and being read have become a common feature of contemporary life in the United States. The universe looks for and takes advantage of every opportunity—no matter how seemingly trivial or trite—to nudge, edge, aid, and guide us. Hence the wisdom of being open and available, keeping our eyes and ears out for our own best selves trying to have a good word with us. Owning and displaying the ability to access extrasensory information about others requires a degree of confidence that many careful and principled individuals do not readily claim. Using available mechanisms to read for oneself, though, is an altogether different matter. It appears that through self-readings, many people are maintaining conscious touch with the movement of divine energies in their lives and are doing so in a way that empowers their sense of themselves as, for lack of a better term, spiritually proficient human beings.

Around 1980, I began using the I Ching. I approached it sparingly, with ceremonial respect and, unlike friends who are confused by its foreign symbolism and non-prescriptive advice, I have always felt that I understood what was being told to me. More recently, I have not thrown the coins as much as I used to. Into that void, as a birthday gift a few years ago, my son gave me a set of Angel Cards. First marketed in 1981 (again, the pivotal early 1980s), each of these fifty-two cards invokes a positive quality such as willingness, communication, faith, humor, tenderness, sisterhood/brotherhood, delight, balance, power, enthusiasm, gratitude, openness, trust, freedom, efficiency, creativity, release, strength, obedience, joy. This quality, rendered in beautiful calligraphy, appears on the card along with one or more colorful angels illustrating that quality in perfect and picturesque ways.

When Adrian's gift arrived in the mail, it was a few days late and, even though he had telephoned loving wishes, I was still miffed about his not getting it to me on time. Inclined as I was in this mood toward non-receptivity, I challenged the cards as soon as I opened them to say something worthwhile to me to prove themselves—without even reading what they were about or looking through them. The card I pulled was FLEXIBIL-ITY, which told me: loosen up your judgment and your attitude, give the kid a break, why don't you, he's struggling through graduate school, with a ton of work and worry, papers and deadlines and a toddler son all on his head. And thus it went every time I have used them—so much so that, at this point, I pull a card each day to help give me inner direction and an uplifting quality to cultivate.

On the day that I conceived the first plan for this particular chapter, the word was INSPIRATION. This card depicts a lavender-robed angel with red wings who stands before an easel, paintbrush in hand, a magnificent golden-green sunrise floating on the canvas and the distant horizon. That day was also the day that I cleared room in my crowded closet and set up a sacred space to remind myself, as Julia Cameron, author of *The Artist's Way* put it, that "creativity is a spiritual, not an ego, thing." Clearly, I was being encouraged to move further forward with my project and to tap into divine aid for some necessary assistance.

Once African American women begin to use spiritual power as a political force, creativity opens. Spirituality can then become for us and, I believe, for everyone who uses it in this conscious and responsible way, an extremely rich source for the creative.

ℳ 4 ℳ

BRINGING BEAUTY
FROM ABOVE:
SPIRITUALITY AND CREATIVITY

At the same time that we burst into a new spirituality around 1980, black women also became noticeably more creative. This is not surprising, for when relationship is established with the all-encompassing, life-giving energy of the universe, enhanced productivity usually follows. The realm of spirit is birthplace for the splendid originality that germinates new ideas in every field, wonderful artistic creations, and lives lived in a lovely fashion. Often, too, inspiration from the spiritual world comes through in specific forms.

Poet Dolores Kendrick and novelist Alice Walker composed literary works through contact with otherworldly ideas and voices. Trying to understand how this happens, what it means, and what the implications are illuminates the authors' own particular processes and the creative process in general. For example, when Alice leaned into her memory to capture the "Celie-voice" of her step-grandmother for *The Color Purple,* she tapped into what she called the "Celie-ness" of women past and present all over the globe. In similar fashion, for her art, Michele Gibbs journeyed within herself to produce drawings that possess enough force to change spiritual life and material conditions. Finally, because of what she reveals about how she wrote her novel *The Salt Eaters,* Toni Cade Bambara forces us to think about creativity as an altered state and about the parallel altering of consciousness that the consumer of the creative product must likewise achieve in order to truly grasp what has been produced.

Dolores and Alice have written books that were assisted by ancestral black women from the realm of spirit. The upsurge of this phenomenon around 1980 represents one of the most important ways that African American women participated in bringing into general consciousness the heightened energies becoming available at that time. Michele grounded her visual art in another culture of color, indigenous Mexico, while Toni pushed vocal black language into the heart of spiritual silence. What was initiated in the early 1980s has continued to flourish. This creative work of black American women shows how functioning spirituality flowers into beauty and power.

In Creative Partnership with Spirit

One night, Dolores, who is usually a good sleeper, could not fall asleep. Getting up at 3:00 A.M., she made a cup of tea and began reading the slave narratives in Gerda Lerner's documentary history, *Black Women in White America.* She became totally immersed and was particularly ensnared by the story of Margaret Garner, a woman who, in 1856, after an unsuccessful escape for freedom, slit the throat of one of her daughters and attempted to kill herself and three of her other children rather than be re-enslaved. This is the same harrowing story from which Toni Morrison's novel *Beloved* germinated. Dolores awoke the next morning with an insistent urge to write a poem based on the Margaret Garner incident. Beyond this, the voice of the woman was coming to her "loud and clear," even though she had had no previous experience with that mode of writing. The voice spoke in dialect and used words with which Dolores was not familiar:

> Cain't cry, 'cause I be dead,
> this old tarp 'round me,
> my flesh rottin,' my bones
> dryin' out, my eyes movin'
> through some kind of cheesecloth,
> like a fog.

Dolores did not know that "tarp" was short for "tarpaulin" until she found it in the dictionary. So, she wrote down tarpaulin, but then realized that, no, this was a slave woman talking and she should simply listen to what she said. She decided "not to fight it," to "just go and follow what I heard."

Thus began a process whereby Dolores sat down with a stack of narratives by black female slaves on her lap, read them with intense emotional involvement, and then "let the voices work" within her. What eventuated was her 1989 poetry collection, *The Women of Plums: Poems in the Voices of Slave Women*. Although Dolores had long conceived of poetry as "a living force capable of working in everybody's life," she had not produced anything as extraordinary as this book. Nor had she channeled voices from the spirit world. She believes that it may take years of preparation of one's spiritual self to be ready for that sort of experience, and she says that she herself would not have been prepared any sooner. For Dolores, years of contemplative living had rendered her open to receive the voices when they came:

I started that kind of life when I was quite young. I was a great one for going off on retreats and being alone. In fact, I have a whole book of spiritual writings, journals I have done in search of the soul, dealing with one's connection to God and the universe. I've been doing this for a long, long, long, long time. And my mother was very much that way. She raised us to believe in it and not to be afraid of that sort of thing. I just accepted it as a way of life and was extremely comfortable with it. I remember girls in college talking about parties and how strange I was because I liked to be by myself. They would say, "How can you stand being by yourself?" And I'd think, "How can you stand not being by yourself?"

Now, as a mature adult, Dolores has "no problems with whatever inner voices are in [her]," and she is growing even stronger in "contemplative prayer, in which you just sit and listen." She also spends a part of every summer writing at a Benedictine monastery in Boulder, Colorado. And, although she is not a practicing spiritualist of any type, Dolores had sensed unseen presences on two or three previous occasions. She opines that these "may have been introductions to opening parts of me that I didn't know were there."

After her first Margaret Garner-inspired hearing, she decided "not to go entirely on instincts" but to conduct some focused historical research. Essentially, however, her writing process remained the same:

Basically, I would sit down with this package of narratives and some of my research notes and I'd read them. Some of them became very painful. I began either to get angry or to come out of it crying, so I had to decide just what I was going to do.

Not wanting to write "history" or "angry poetry," she fixed on the strength of slave women, thinking about how they and the women in her own family belied the demeaning media images of African American women as shallow, stupid, grossly unfeminine, blindly nurturing, or sexually voracious. Ultimately, Dolores has decided that she "summoned" the "women of plums" through the historical documents:

I would read them and some I would deal with and some I wouldn't. I got the historical outline of the character, who the person was, or the narrative, and then I would put it aside and sit down and begin to write. Now what is she saying? What is she really saying? What is the voice here? Once I got the idea of the woman in my head, I began to sit down and write the narrative in her voice, in what I was hearing from her, not in terms of who I was.

Dolores sees her role as giving voice to women who had not been able to speak for a hundred years, but admits that she cannot totally explain the "mechanics":

We know very little about the creative process. This experience has taught me that. I've always believed that I as an artist am a vehicle through which the creative energy flows, and that that links me with God. I thoroughly believe that. I don't believe I originate anything. I think God originates it and He in His wisdom has given tons of people on this planet certain talents through which they can bring their art to the surface. I think I saw that manifested very, very strongly in this particular work, and I don't understand it. And I'm not going to try to understand it. I'm just going to try to accept it because I think that there is a level of creativity that people hit that we know very little about.

Dolores hit the level of creative accomplishment that she reached in *The Women of Plums* because the slave women were coming through to her, in her earlier words, "loud and clear." They were women with authentically original names like Ndzeli, Leah, Peggy, Sophie, Bethany Veney, Prunella, Jenny, Hattie, Rya, Juba, Lula, Lucy, Polly, Aunt Mary, Liza Lily, Jo, Sidney, Lottie, Anne, Julia, Gravity, Harriet, Miss Maggie, Cora Sue, Tildy, Althea, Emma, Aunt Sarah, Vera, and Sadie. Insistently and vociferously, these heretofore silent but now spiritually emancipated women were recounting bits and pieces of their strenuous lives, telling stories that had not been told before about running away from slavery, having a picnic with a dead best friend, being in love, being prostituted to white men by the master when he needed extra money, praying on the auction block to be bought with daughter and not separately, nursing the Civil War soldiers on both sides of the conflict, sleeping with the master, being beaten, being abandoned, singing lullabies to a downcast child, and so on.

And they spoke in voices that were engaged, impassioned, quintessentially human. Here is the way Margaret Garner, called Peggy, explains why she was willing to kill herself and her children rather than be re-enslaved:

> *. . . I tried to escape*
> *from they dark breaths,*
> *they glories, hallelujahs!*
> *they fine houses and sweet fields,*
> *they murders murders murders!*
> *they coffins stenchin' in they smiles,*
> *they come heah Peggy,*
> *dress my little one,*
> *then fix her somethin' to eat,*
> *maybe some cake and milk,*
> *and mine sittin' on the stairs*
> *in the cold, in the dark,*
> *waitin' to do some waitin' on*
> *waitin' for the milk to sour*
> *and the cake to crumble,*
> *hearin' all this*
> *without a word, a whimper,*
> *eyes freezin' in they dreams,*
> *hungers freezin' in they dark,*
> *takin' they dreams to supper*
> *like candles meltin,'*
> *after 'while no more light,*
> *they walkin' softly*
> *makin' sure they seen and not heard*
> *and they dreams screamin'*
> *in they bright, soft eyes.*

With her discerning mind, in her strong, soft African American dialect, Margaret Garner makes us see just how untenable this life of slavery had become for her—its fine, smiling surface but stinking underside, its constant on-call servitude, its pampering of white children and freezing of black children's dreams. Whether anybody had ever recorded it or not, we know, for instance, that slave boys and girls waited on cold, dark stairs to spring into service on command. We also sense in these lines a different time and place and an unfamiliar plane of reality. Dolores's supernatural accessing of Margaret's voice puts us in direct contact with another—the astral—world, especially in eerie statements such as:

> . . . I burn and burn
> all inside
> turn to dust
> blow away out over
> they heads when they
> finds me cryin' in a sack.

or:

> I'm travelin' in my bones
> and the Spirit swooshes out
> before I gets a chance to say
> Amen.

Most of Dolores's commentary on the poems documents the degree to which she was not in complete control of their composition, and she jokingly says that she sometimes felt the women were standing in line crying, "My turn, my turn." Dolores mentions Jenny as an example. She brought nice short pieces, but would show up only when she wanted to and not when Dolores called on her for a small poem. "Prunella's Picnic" is another instance of how the work assumed a life of its own that Dolores herself did not always comprehend. Not until she had finished writing the poem did she realize that Prunella's friend was no longer alive.

> [Prunella] was in this kitchen talking to her friend, surviving through talking to her—and she's talking about having a picnic. And I thought, "How can she be having a picnic in the kitchen?" But then it went and it developed. At the end of the poem I looked and I said, "My God, she's dead. Tula is dead."

Reflecting back on the process of *The Women of Plums,* Dolores has decided that she would not want to write another such book—even though she would accept it if it happened again: "I'm just saying that I'm not going out looking for it. I would not sit in a room at night and conjure these people up and say, 'Now, I need some more of you to speak to me.' I would never do that." Her reason is that the experience was too painful, even though she knew that the women were saying "that they triumphed in the end." The ordeal of not being "yourself," of being "something else" in the service of mediumship was also exhausting enough for her to finally stop the process: "I know that whenever you move into this realm, you are using psychic energy that you didn't even know you had. I didn't know if I had any more left and I didn't want to find out. So I just let it go."

Dolores's discussion of her writing in terms of "being yourself" versus being "something else" illustrates the fact that creativity can be thought of as emanating from two basic places—

one being the artist, and the other being the overshadowing in-spirational energy that she calls "God." This issue resurfaced when I spoke with Alice Walker about the genesis of her famous 1982 novel, *The Color Purple.* I went into the conversation thor-oughly influenced by the remarks she had made that seemed to say that the work was a channeled creation, that is, one that was practically dictated from some higher source to and through her.

At the end of the book, for instance, she refers to herself as "A. W., author and medium" and thanks all the characters for "coming." Also, in widespread, published accounts, she amusingly talks about how the characters came to her for her to tell their story. She says that in order to find a place to live that the charac-ters liked, she was compelled to move from New York City, to Brooklyn, to San Francisco, and finally to Mendocino County in northern California. They had complained to her about noise, tall buildings, and crowded buses and said things like, San Fran-cisco is "pretty, but us ain't lost nothing in no place that has earthquakes." When she settled into a place that reminded them of their home town in rural Georgia, where they could see sheep and cattle, smell hay and apples, the characters, according to Alice, "began, haltingly, to speak."

This explanation of the novel's genesis rang true for me be-cause of the strong and unusual reaction it had aroused in me. Having spent my life as an introverted child with my "head in a book" and later as an English major, I had read hundreds of texts. None, however, had affected me in quite the way that *The Color Purple* did. Even now, I remember exactly where I was when I finished reading it, and I can feel again my immediate emotions. I was tingly and a little breathless, and, beyond that, totally sad to be done with the novel because it meant no more contact with the people in it. I wrote Alice a letter that was the closest thing to "fan mail" I have ever produced. Then I moped around for a few weeks, unable to get interested in any other books because they paled in comparison with the shimmer and energy of the one I had just put down.

Given this personal experience and Alice's origins story, I therefore began our interview by asking Alice Walker to speak about her creative process for *The Color Purple,* and particularly about the characters coming to her. Immediately, she aimed her response at correcting the view of her novel as a mediumistic or channeled work:

> Let me explain something, because I'm not a channel. I don't channel. What I do is work really, really hard to try to understand. . . . What I meant when I said "medium" is that by the time I had done the work that I needed to do, just in preparing myself, including moving my own body from one part of the world to another, they [the characters] were completely real to me. So it was as if they came to me. It wasn't as if they just descended. In other words, creativity of this sort is very much like making love. To be a really excellent lover means to serve the person you love, and to do it with your whole heart. You do whatever has to be done to serve and to love that person because you love them. It's no different from writing a book about people that you truly love. You want to serve them, and you want to do it as well as you can. There is a time at which—as in lovemaking—a miracle happens, and they come.

She explained that some of the characters are, in fact, based on actual people she knew whose histories she simply rewrote as fiction. Alice said she was "delighted" that I was raising these questions, "because somebody has really needed to get this straight for a long time," and then she differentiated between her process and being a channel:

> The difference is that a channel is an empty space. You deliberately make yourself empty so that other things can fill you and go through you. And this is all very wonderful. However, the difference is that I am there, too, and I am very conscious of being there. So that what I'm working on meets in me and merges with me, and that is what happens, rather than people just coming through totally as themselves and with none of me in them.

When she writes, she gets "extremely passionate" about what she is creating. She devotes herself to her art "in the same way that you would to a religion" (a very direct equating of creativity and spirituality), and she calls on "all the ancestors" for support. They respond, *Alice, hard work.*

As I pushed for greater clarity, Alice illustrated her response by using Celie, the main character from *The Color Purple.* Celie was based on Alice's stepgrandmother, a southern, black, country woman who was married off to her grandfather and birthed two children who died, a woman who really did not herself "have a life." Alice felt it was her job as an educated person and an artist to "free the spirit inside her [stepgrandmother]," to "liberate her from that history of being 'nobody'":

> ***Alice:*** And I understood, writing along with this, that it was bigger than me. I really did know that the creativity

had taken fire, that it was moving as if it had real help and support. Now the fuel for that was love.

Akasha: Whose love?

Alice: Mine. It was my love of Celie as my grandmother who was jumping over the fence finally, getting away. . . . There were so many days when I just chuckled because I could just see her and feel her coming to life as a spiritual being.

Akasha: And would you say at that point you were in touch with the energy that was manifested specifically as her in her lifetime?

Alice: Well, I could say "possibly." But here is the wonderful thing. The wonderful thing about life is that if you can find the spirit in yourself, an identifiable spiritual reality in yourself, somebody's been born that fits it exactly. . . . So since that is true, I felt, well, who knows whether this is really the spirit that would have flourished in her!

Akasha: Or was her.

Alice: Or was her. I mean, it definitely wasn't the one that I saw, wasn't the stepgrandmother that I knew. Celie is not. But she's someone. So I would imagine that she is partly me, she is partly her [the stepgrandmother], she is partly whoever is that spirit which I was able to express.

Alice asserts that this Celie-ness, this spirit energy is recognized by "all the Celies of the world," no matter their present stage of personal oppression or liberation, whether they are in India or Pakistan, Iceland or Germany—because they write to her and say, "That's me." However, "the underlying thing is what we've always said in our culture: the spirit doesn't die."

When Alice began creating Celie and thinking about her stepgrandmother, all she had to go on was the one thing her grandmother had left—her voice:

> So I would lean toward my memory of her sound and try really hard but gently just to get any little sentence, any little word, any little expression, any little grunt. And for that—I mean, to get one of my stepgrandmother's grunts in a clear way—is why I had to move from New York to California and go into the country, because I needed to be able to really hear it. I couldn't hear it anywhere else, other than in real peace and silence. . . . But after I could remember her saying, "Sho do," you know, I could make up, could say anything and it would sound like how she would say it. And at that point it would be so real that to me it would feel like she had just taken wing and that she was talking.

When I asked her how that happened, she responded: "Well, I think you become the person you create, for the period of time that you're doing it." The trick, Alice said, is to keep one's own ego and limitations out of the way so that, for instance, anything Celie said would "*always* be what she was saying, *always* be what she would do, and *never* what you would say or what you would do." This utter detachment became possible because, in Alice's own words:

I just loved Celie too much to try to take away from her in any way. I mean, it's so simple, simplistic, maybe simple-minded, whatever, but it's just love. That's all it is. And when you feel it for whomever or whatever, it's not a difficult thing to just step out of the way and understand your role as someone who's serving this person.

Many years of apprenticeship, many years of work provide the requisite skill—in the same way that a musician spends a decade playing scales and then begins to fly.

How Creative Love and Help Come from Above

These discussions with Dolores and Alice take on extremely thorny and delicate issues relating to creativity, issues that have been spoken about in various ways by myriad people over centuries of time. To wend my way through what they say, I have a way of thinking about these matters that helps me personally to explain what would otherwise be beyond explanation. As one point of departure, we can begin with Dolores's account of hearing "loud and clear" the voices of *The Women of Plums*. If we take her report at face value (and there is no reason why we should not), then we have to ask: How would such a mode of communication and writing occur?

To answer this question, I begin with the consideration that our usual conception of *aliveness* means that consciousness is inhabiting a body made up of physical, emotional, and mental aspects. As I understand it, the consciousness thread is connected to these three parts. When we sleep, for instance, consciousness withdraws from the physical body, including the brain, and inhabits the other two components. These components are the realms from where dreams and other things that we do not *know* we know come. The problem is that our bigger consciousness knows these things, but *we*—in our physical brain—do not, not unless and until our mind can impress them on the brain. We get bits of this information from what we remember of our dreams. We also apprehend it in those rare moments of unexplainable lucidity, of intuition, and flashes of knowing that seem to come from nowhere.

When we "die," our consciousness eventually withdraws from all three parts of our material self—physical-emotional-mental—but that consciousness continues to exist on even higher planes. This higher existence is the aspect of our selves that many people term soul, or spirit. And, like everything else in the universe, it is energy and never dies—it just exists in varying forms. In recent years, a large number of books about near-death experiences have been published. Individuals who have had these experiences always report seeing the thread of life-consciousness and, at the end of it, a tunnel of light.

From the spirit or divine realm, souls-spirits *out* of bodies can communicate with souls-spirits *in* bodies, with those of us who are, for the moment, incarnate on the physical plane. This seems to happen most readily when souls, or spirits, are just leaving or just returning to Earth. And this communication is also something we tend to become aware of most easily when we are in the astral world of sleep and dreams, or otherwise tapping into that generally unconscious part of our larger selves, whether through intense concentration, meditation, trance, or other altered states. Certainly, then, it is plausible to entertain the idea that people in spirit form could communicate with authors—telling their life stories, or imparting other knowledge acquired since they left the limited plane of the lower, sensory world and now have more universal awareness.

I wholeheartedly embrace the idea that, as Dolores put it, an artist is "a vehicle through which the creative energy flows," and that this is a link to or sameness with God. However, experience has taught me that while it is one thing to contact this energy and even to consciously register its messages and meaning, it is quite another matter to fashion what has been received into concrete form. For me, this book is a case in point. I knew what it was supposed to do, how it should feel, could almost, one might say, taste it, but it wasn't until years of groping and rewriting had passed that I felt I had finally gotten it right, and this feeling, now that I think about it, had to do with hearing, being in touch with the same faculty of voice and ear that was crucial for Dolores and Alice.

With regard to this issue of how difficult it is to concretely materialize what has been received from the immaterial world, Alice's remarks about her creation of Celie provide necessary perspective. Once the world of spiritual ideas—encapsulated, for example, in the concept of a collective "Celie-ness"—is contacted, the artist melds this "channeling" with and through her own personal talent. By contrast, a medium is a passive instrument, one who gives over her body, mind, and voice for the use of some being without a body. This passive channeling is the kind of mediumship that Alice wishes to distance herself from— and understandably so. In certain respects, it is a feminist issue.

Most of the famous and not-so-famous trance mediums of the nineteenth century were girls and young women, often slight of build and constitutionally frail. They were being used as vehicles or carriers in a stereotypically subjugated-female way. Furthermore, for contemporary women writers, and especially African American ones, who are boldly claiming voice, self, and power, it would be unpalatable to say that they had nothing to do with the writing of their work, that no art or craft from themselves was involved or necessary. We can note that Alice signed *The Color Purple*, "*author* and medium" [my emphasis]. She claims her due at the same time as she admits that it is also bigger than her personal self.

In any event, bypassing or giving up one's mind would not be a good thing, for the mind is the instrument that can be used to knowingly and deliberately contact our own soul-spirit and the larger realm of soul-spirit of which that is a part. In that region is contained all knowledge, all creativity. Physicist Paul Davies names this in the title of his book: *The Mind of God*, the source of the good, the true, and the beautiful. This is the place that mystics, meditators, and metaphysicians reach. It is where great breakthroughs in science and art come from. Once the mind contacts this plane of ideas and images, however, the clarity and beauty with which what is perceived gets "brought down to Earth" and wrought in some form—a novel, a theorem, a painting, a poem, a symphony—depends on the person. Here is where the individual's intelligence-training-skill-knowledge-discipline, ability to discriminate, ability to express, come into play. This is the part of the process that "author" Alice Walker rightfully wants to hold on to and give herself credit for, even as she continues to closely link herself and her work with ancestral spirits.

For both Alice and Dolores, it was black women from the past who became present to them, their contemporary descendants. These black female ancestral spirits carried various agendas. They wanted to have their heretofore untold life stories recorded. They needed to have their existences validated and redeemed. They came when called to provide assistance, inspiration, and support for creative work that would benefit their immediate successors and the world. The invocative and evocative medium was voice, harking back to the African concept of *nommo*, which is "the power of the word and the receiving ear." Writers are, in critical respects, listeners. They are poised to hear, and they are also in the position to pass on whatever comes to them—a factor which explains why the appearances to these authors were so insistent and strong. I have no doubt that supra-human forces and energies have always aided "worthy" writers. However, cloaked under generic theories of inspiration and the muse's skirt, their identity has not always been explicitly named.

A feature of the contemporary black-female literary scene is that more and more women writers are opting to talk openly about the concretely metaphysical places their characters and stories come from. This includes a giant like Toni Morrison who spoke in a conversation with sister writer Gloria Naylor about her necessity "to have now very overt conversations" with Sethe (from her celebrated novel, *Beloved*) and her other characters. As Toni put it:

> Before, I could sort of let it disguise itself as the artist's monologue with herself, but there's no time for that foolishness now. Now I have to call them by their names and ask them to reappear and tell me something or leave me alone even.

People are often embarrassed, fearful, distrustful, or silent about the place a writer enters to meet these characters, but Morrison thinks that writers opening up about this will help others open up as well:

> I think the more black women write, the more easily one will be able to talk about those things. . . . People speak, of course, of the muse and there are other words for this [process of creation]. But to make it as graphic a presence or a collection of presences as I find it absolutely to be, it's not even a question of trying to make it that way—that's the way that it appears. There are not a lot of people to whom one speaks that way. But I know that that's what it is. It isn't a question of searching it out. It's a question of my perceptions and in that area, I know.

Having intimate contact with ancestral spirits, combined with their own authorial mandates, seems to be making it easier for African American women writers to play the role of lifting up this aspect of the creative process for others to view, hopefully in a way that will give everyone permission to speak more clearly.

The flurry of such activity occurring from the late 1970s and early 1980s until the present suggests the advent of a closer rapport between our earthly, physical plane and the more spiritual realms. This would be in line with evolutionary progression and, specifically, with the gathering energies of the immediate New Age. It seems that forces from these higher realms are concerned with aiding and assisting us during these trying, pivotal times. Perhaps we are being helped to remember who we really are and, as African shaman Malidoma Somé put it, where we have come from in order to fulfill our duties on this Earth. Perhaps we are being helped to know that we have the personal and spiritual resources we need, that we are stronger and greater than the human problems that we, in touch with our spiritual being, can overcome.

Painting with an Open Hand

So far I have discussed spirituality and creativity in terms of a poet and a novelist, women whose medium is language and the written word. Creativity, of course, manifests in all art forms and, beyond that, can brilliantly color every daily act. Lucille Clifton indirectly made this point. When she spoke about writing poems, making it seem as if it were a natural process of simply allowing something to happen, I said to her, "You sound like you think everybody can write poetry." She replied,

> I think everybody can express. I know everybody wants to. I know there is in humans a great urge toward expressing that ineffable thing that is a part of us. I think some people do it with poems and I know people that can cornrow pretty close to it. I think that people tend not to listen. It's educated out of you. My luck is that I wasn't that educated.

When artist Michele Gibbs discusses her paintings, she takes us into another medium of creative expression—closer to a tactile and visual art form such as cornrowing. However, everything she says continues to link spirituality with creativity at the same time that it proves that creativity is not dependent on "education" or rationality for its being—in the same way that spirituality happens outside of or beyond the accustomed order of reality.

Michele begins her story of how she took both her spirituality and her art to a higher level at the point where she left Detroit with her husband, George. They were both unusually ferment-oriented social activists who found themselves ready for major changes in their life. They decided to go and live in Mexico, with indigenous people of this hemisphere who had been colonized, exploited, and oppressed, but who had survived. She says, "It was an entirely different energy that they had, and since they were still around, they must know something since the extermination process had certainly been more severe in their case than in ours [African Americans]." She and George settled on Oaxaca, one of the poorest states with one of the highest percentages of indigenous people. Sure enough, what they found was "a clear power space with totally different energy."

This clear power space in Oaxaca opened up Michele artistically and literally opened the door to the material for her art, which turned out to be *amate*, the sacred, pre-Colombian pressed wood bark of the Central American timber tree *Ficus glabrata* that was used historically by the Indians to ceremoniously record their codices and cosmology. Having come in contact with this material fifteen years previously, she had always wanted to work with it. Now she was able to secure ample quantities of the amate, engage meditatively and creatively with it, and thereby produce paintings that were a radical departure from her previous work and from the way the material was utilized by the native artists. Being in Oaxaca made all of this possible because, not only was it a center of magical realism for visual artists, it was also one of the only two places in the world where people still made amate in the traditional way. Michele knew none of this before she arrived. It was for her, blessedly, a matter of being available and being led in the right direction, just as was finding the perfect house in which to live: "A hexagon facing east with lots of archways." To this Michele said, "Right. Someone has me in mind. I don't have to build my own house after all. It's here already. Thank you, thank you!"

Everything in Oaxaca was like this. Michele says, "It has cleared me out wonderfully to live there. And it has changed my artistic process, as well as the way it looks when it comes out." In the United States, Michele worked with the graphic arts, black and white, as clear and unambiguous as possible, because she wanted to bring people face to face with their condition and shock them into doing something about it—the kind of art that corresponded with her confrontational, political organizing. Using amate resulted in work that was completely different. For Michele,

> amate is a material that reflects the substance it comes from. It's the pressed bark of the wild fig tree. After it's pressed, you still see the grain of the wood, the bark. You still have the memory, to use that word, of the natural organic form. And meditating on what that memory holds became the source of the images I tried to excavate.

Just as voices came to the women writers I spoke with, visual images came to the artist Michele. Within three months, she had produced an astonishing sixty pieces of art. She says, "I was possessed. I was totally taken by this process." Shortly thereafter, at an exhibit of her work, Mexican and Indian artists were surprised and pleased by her art, by the fact that she was using the amate as more than just a surface upon which to paint. Her method gave them new ideas about how to approach their work, and forged connections between them and Michele that continue to grow as they interact in their shared artistic community.

As our discussion continued, I asked Michele to expand upon

the process of meditating on the amate and having the images and the painting emerge:

> *Michele:* First of all, it's a very collaborative process between me and the material. If you let the material be your only guide, which is to say if you simply use all the images that you see in the texture of the bark, it will be too much. It will not have a coherent form.

> *Akasha:* Okay, so you're meditating on this amate, and the swirls and whirls and the dark and light and the lines and so forth become like a moving sea of faces and figures and grounds and landscapes. Is that how it goes?

> *Michele:* Yes. First it comes to you and then you have to go to it because . . . well, this is very difficult for me.

> *Akasha:* To talk about?

> *Michele:* To do! I'm an Aries, very willful.

What she instinctively wants is to impose her will on the material. The lesson she struggles to learn—evident ever since her traumatic experience working with the Grenada revolution that ended when the U.S. military invaded in 1983—is patience and "the limits of will, negative will, in this case power as domination. It led me to read Bessie Head [the celebrated South African writer], and it led me in a direction of exploration internally and externally that made me ready to use this new material, this old new material in the way that I think it deserves to be used."

Not surprisingly, the specifics of how she works all aim at getting herself, her ego-personality self out of the way even as that self is allied with the "idea" that wants to come through:

Michele: It's first thing in the morning, and I'm out in the sunshine. And depending on what I've dreamed the night before, or what article I've read, or what my rational, articulated concerns are at that point, I put on a piece of music. And then, between the music and the sunshine and the bark, I try to see what goes there.

Akasha: You try to see what, of all that's there, needs to be brought out.

Michele: What of all that's there I could use. How much of this can I use, as Audre Lorde says.

Akasha: So you begin to get some of that foreground itself. And is there a thing you do with your mind so that you sort of, like, suppress the images that you aren't going to bring out?

Michele: Yeah, I take my glasses off! I don't focus there. No problem!

Akasha: How funny! So you take your glasses off, and then, since you're tuned in, you can see the thing that you're going to . . .

Michele: The main part; leave the rest alone.

Akasha: And then what do you do?

Michele: I just draw, I just work with it.

However, instead of immediately reaching for her pen (which is her old habit as a skilled draftsperson), Michele forces herself to concentrate not on line but on *areas* of color and shape and their suggestiveness, then she works toward blocking these out: "If there is a mountain range, and I can see where it starts, but I don't know where it stops—I start with the *colors* of the mountain and the sky and let that lead into whatever is in the foreground, and then, as a second step, after the outer whole has taken shape, move into the interior with line and specificity."

We can recall that Dolores and Alice, as writers, refused to be viewed simply as channels and mediums, and they insisted on acknowledging the parts they consciously played in their own creative processes. Michele's description of the way she produces her art echoes this. She speaks about her methodology as "collaboration" and states that she cannot let the material be her "only guide," which would be analogous to permitting voices to totally dictate and prescribe. Instead and in addition, she has to use her own talent and resources, skill and judgment to give the images, the "messages," what she terms "coherent form." In a seeming paradox, this is occurring even as she sets herself aside so as to be able to see what needs seeing unobstructed and undistorted by her own individual will and agendas.

Spirituality, spiritual consciousness, a spiritual practice enables all of us—like Michele, like other African American women artists—to enter into creativity and to maintain the detachment and discipline required to manifest what we find there.

Reading as Creation: Another Altered State

Just as the creative process involves making contact with the universe of spirit, so can the process of imbibing the creative product. Looking at Toni Cade Bambara's *The Salt Eaters* from both sides of the paradigm—that is, from the perspective of both the writer and the reader—shows clearly how this dual enterprise works. What Toni says about how she created the novel emphasizes that she was writing from a spiritual dimension outside her normal, everyday, rational self. So, as readers, how, then, do we make sense of what came to its creator "beyond sense," so to speak? What can we as ordinary mortals (or predominantly in our ordinary mortal consciousness) be expected to garner or expect ourselves to garner from such an artifact?

Toni began our discussion of her writing *The Salt Eaters* with the self-framed question of, "Why do a book like that?" Her answer:

> I do a book like that because I need to get to my next step, and I was revving the motor and not having clarity. I was wrenching away from what I was supposed to be doing. So I said, "Okay, then sit the fuck down and gather yourself together, pull yourself in." And when I pull myself in, that is what it looks like.

At other times, she might have gathered herself by singing or dancing it out with a group or scripting it for community theater. But because she was engaged in writing, the process became a novel. While working on it, she was, as she put it, "in that chamber of myself that I trust, where I go down to test whether something is bogus, or for me, or whatever." That chamber is the part of oneself that is clean and can be trusted to reveal to you—often in dreamtime—the collusion with the unacceptable that you might have made during the day. *Salt* comes out of that place "almost"—a place that does not concern itself with "common, rational, mundane" things. Creating from that "pure" place, Toni says that she does not remember much.

I mean, I quickly forgot as soon as I could the experience of writing that book. It was not easy; it was very painful and very annoying. I lost a lot of friends, so I wanted to move on. I don't remember, nor did I record much about the process either. I was just mostly interested in getting it done.

To paraphrase Toni Cade Bambara, she was grateful that her editor, Toni Morrison, did not bother her, except to occasionally drift over her "brain pan" a brilliant or wonderful idea—and then leave it to her to act on it or not, depending on whether it felt right to her. Toni concludes: "I didn't know what I was doing, but I knew it was all right to do it."

When I tried to have her expand on not knowing what she was doing, as she put it, we both agreed that we did not mean anything as specific or detailed as an outline for all twelve chapters of the book:

Toni: But I mean a general law, the general map. No one embarks on a novel without some notes, without an outline, without some dry runs, without some chunks, without some vision of the whole, some notion of that last scene, or some . . .

Akasha: Right, but you had none of that.

Toni: Not in that way, no. Not in that way.

Akasha: Okay, see, that's what I want you to talk about. In what way did you have it? And in what way *did* it come out?

Toni: Oh, we don't have no language, we have no language for that.

Akasha: See, that's what I *really* wish you would talk about.

Toni: There's nothing to talk about. That's what I mean. It's not a talking thing. You feel it and you do it. It absolutely is not a talking thing. You have a motive, you have a drive, and you've got a repertoire, you've got resources. And you have something else: permission to do it.

Akasha: Yes, from the gods.

Toni: And that's finally what you have, that's it. That's really it.

Once an author has this permission, what triggers or feeds the work becomes the only issue. With *Salt,* Toni had a short story she was writing about an old slave insurrection "that was plaguing me, getting fatter and sprawlier and shaggier, and a motive, which was to pull in. And they came together and they developed." Each person, each character, attached "like a little polyp" to ideas she wanted to explore.

We can understand somewhat better what Toni meant about the process not being "a talking thing" when we ponder her observation that she reads the book in the same way that I or any other person does, and that she is "continually discovering texts within that text." Like most readers, she also can "never find" particular passages that she is looking for, although she did "very little rearranging." Even though *The Salt Eaters* is given narrative focus by the communal healing at its center, the novel is constructed in a holistic, organic style that mimetically replicates the enmeshed, intertwined, holographic nature of the universe. Because of this fact, knowing the characters and events and how the plot moves and interconnects is no guarantee that one can turn to a precisely remembered passage, for the text is an accretive unity rather than a linear one. And, further, the various strands and patterns of the novel have a way—like life itself—of presenting themselves in new and ever more complex manifestations. Therefore, someone who has studied the work knows exactly what Toni means when she admits that even she, the author, finds her book changeable, elusive, and new. Truly surprising, though, is what she says in the following quote about not knowing at all some of the things that she has written, using as an example the first law of thermodynamics, which figures prominently in one key section of the book:

> Every time I do read, I read something new. It's new, it's just new: "Oh, I didn't know." It's like when you're dreaming and you know all the characters' motivations, even though the characters are starkly different from your assumed self. And these characters have jobs, professions, and skills you know that you don't know nothing about in daytime, but you definitely know all about at night. So it's that kind of startling: "Well, gee, *hmm*, what is the first law of thermodynamics? I mean, I used to know. I don't know now. What does this mean?" Then I have to get up and think about it, walk around.

Yes, absolutely, the question to ask is, "What does this mean?" I think it means simply what Toni's remarks suggest, that she wrote *The Salt Eaters* in an altered state, in a state that connected her to the universe of spirit. Therefore, out of that state, she would not know—even allowing for ordinary loss of memory—all of what she knew within it. As a science major Toni knew, of course, that the first law of thermodynamics is about the conservation of energy, and its meaning expands into the esoteric concept that energy cannot be created or destroyed. She also brilliantly grasped both its physical and metaphysical implications when she wrote in the novel of Damballah, a popular voodoo deity associated with water, lightning, and the serpent-snake:

> Damballah is the first law of thermodynamics and is the Biblical wisdom and is the law of time and is . . . everything that is now has been before and will be again in a new way, in a changed form, in a timeless time.

From one perspective, Damballah is about the transmutation (symbolized by the snake) of water and fire (lightning) into energy—precisely the combination of ingredients that first gave rise to this law of thermodynamics in the nineteenth century, when technicians for the captains of industry were trying to design steam engines and locomotives that worked more efficiently. The metaphysical implications inherent in this law also lead to the truth of creation and the atemporal eternity of time, and allude to the spiritual idea that the beginning of all existence (whether the big bang of science, or the creationism of Genesis) produced everything that has been, is, or ever will be in a closed system of recycling and protean energy.

These ideas are so richly provocative that even a non-novelist, Roger S. Jones, in his nonfiction book *Physics for the Rest of Us,* waxes rhapsodic about one of their components, fire, which is the element that defines and excites the Aries in Toni. As Jones puts it:

> Promethean fire is far more than physical. It is the brilliant fire of the intellect and imagination, the burning fire of passion, the smoldering fire of envy, the raging

fire of hate, and the infernal fire of destruction. Fire can enlighten, energize, delight, cleanse, purify, inflame, trick, cajole, create, transform, and consume.

Promethean fire is the foundation of science: Chemists and biologists deal constantly with the notions of combustion and oxidation—they even talk of life itself as "slow fire." Fire and heat are the basis of energy and its conservation.

Thus the scientist finds himself in the same realms of energy and the imagination that Toni invokes with the spiritual metaphysics of her handling of the thermodynamics law. In *The Salt Eaters*, the character Campbell (think mythologist Joseph Campbell), who makes the Damballah-thermodynamics statement, is a projection of Toni's own incredibly associative mind. Campbell arrives at this truth in a "flash," in a "glowing moment"—just like the one Toni must have experienced as she was writing her novel—flashes and moments that are not readily or totally translatable into analytical discourse.

When we read, we tend to approach novels with our lower, concrete, rational minds. But, in order to really get *The Salt Eaters*, we need to reach an altered, higher consciousness, just like Toni when she wrote it—or, for those whose metaphors tend in the other direction, we need to reach the below-the-rational consciousness place that is the chamber of pure self. In effect, our process is an act of creation in reverse; we do what she did in the opposite order. She first apprehended an idea and then brought it into language; we must enter language and swim toward the transcendent idea. Once arrived, we find ourselves in her predicament: how to say the *what* we know, describe the spiritual space pulsing all around us.

In inspired *(inspired!)* moments, I can do little bits of this grasping and describing with Toni's brilliant novel, which explains the feeling I had upon finishing my essay on *Salt* in 1981, when I sensed participation in a reality larger than myself to which I had somehow managed not only to ascend, but to contribute. Touching the novel with our best and most receptive selves, we, again holographically speaking, touch the universe it is, the universe it contains. And, yet, in the final analysis, no matter how many words we run around it or how much we bluff language, there is something, still, about the essence of creativity that, as Toni bluntly put it, "is not a talking thing." Lucille Clifton quotes the poet Carolyn Forché: "The language of God is silence." Paradoxes abound and astound. A voluble black sister like Toni whose writerly trademark is voice transports us all to a place where we pick up the absolutely stunning and sacred sound of silence, the space of the all-creative.

5

WORKING TO REDEEM THE PLANET:
SPIRITUALITY AND HEALING

Spirituality has become an important tool in the healing of contemporary African American women. It's not that earlier generations of black women left this crucial resource unutilized, but today, because of the consciousness fostered by the civil rights and feminist movements, we more publicly acknowledge the need for healing our wounds, both racial and feminine. When spirituality is brought to bear on the myriad ills that result from the grossly unjust distribution of power and privilege in this country, then necessary kinds of healing can begin to occur. In addition, a hallmark of the current New Age spiritual movement, a hallmark that has proven to be highly influential and popular, is the quest to attain optimum physical, emotional, mental, and psychic health.

Because racial and gender oppression begin at birth, much of this healing and optimizing for black women involves traversing painful childhood territory. As children, many of us experienced feeling different, being isolated, and, as a result, becoming exceptionally introspective—negative experiences which, nevertheless, simultaneously fostered some countervailing strengths. Thrown back upon our young selves and our inner resources, when we did not go under, we developed an impressive list of positive assets that include: original thought and creative imagination; independence and self-reliance; awareness of spiritual beings and energies; a sense of a core divine self that could not be beaten down or killed. These are all qualities with spiritual relevance and resonance that seem to have disposed many African American women toward spiritual paths.

For instance, where I am in my life at this moment as an increasingly happy and truly self-confident person has everything to do with my commitment to confronting my early history of sexual and emotional abuse and finally being able to see these experiences less as victimization and more as far-reaching redemption. In adulthood, Sonia Sanchez and Namonyah Soipan draw on what they learned, as solitary little girls, about handling spiritual energies. And the waves of self-love and self-affirmation that presently sustain Geraldine McIntosh and Toni Cade Bambara, they trace back to the sense of themselves as essentially "all right," a discovery they were forced to make in their often dysfunctional and eccentric first homes. Despite the fact that our lives may have been difficult, a large number of us have come to realize that these lives we lived were spiritually perfect, that is, that we were placed precisely into those families and circumstances that would grow us into the people we needed to be, the spiritual women we were destined to become.

What I call circumstances include our being women, being black women, being poor women, and/or being sexually abused women. Together and singly these could be regarded as hardships and disabilities. However, these "difficult" identities were transformed into beauty and power by some "grace or message or whim or caring" that could be thought of as the universal divine. That the spiritual energies of the universe can transform in this way is heartening for women of color, who are often dealt more than one challenging hand. Appearances and stereotypes notwithstanding, African American women have been not simply victims or even survivors, but redeemers. In the process of moving through our lives, we have helped impel the ever greater growth of planetary consciousness.

"No Fault": A Story of Personal Pain and Healing

This book began noting that the years 1979 and 1980 inaugurated for me a cycle of conscious spiritual activity that synchronized with the accelerated changes taking place both for other African American women and throughout the world. A second personal growth spurt occurred about seven years later, when I wrote the following poem. The topic of the poem is the sexual abuse of little girls. It starts in an oppressive, accusatory voice intended to mirror the falsely internalized guilt of girls and women, but this perspective is ultimately vanquished by a ceremonial enactment of collective healing. Here is the poem.

No Fault
(for the Circle)

It's your fault, sister
You danced in front of your uncle
when you were three
with just your panties on
So, it's your fault, baby

All your fault—
that your father needed a second wife
*   who looked just like your mother*
that your mother only had
*   her daughter to love*
that your grownup brother
*   took you for a toy*
*   when he was drunk*

That Satan's family
*   wanted a ritual victim*
the neighbor next door
*   a backyard thrill*
that your stepfather really believed
*   he wasn't any kin to you*

That the deacon said God commanded you
*   to be his little angel*
that the people at daycare
*   played mommy-and-daddy*
*   played a nasty pattycake with you*

Remember, it was you who danced
in your baby-pink panties

It's all your fault
that they fondled and patted
        fingered and poked
        rubbed, sucked
        diddled, daddled, and fucked
on you

It's your fault, sister
your fault
It's your fault
The voices, the internal tape
   droning on and on
It's your fault
You know that you did it
So, it's all your fault,
the tapes and the voices
staining deeper and deeper
It's your fault
It's your fault
It's your fault

Sister, woman
Sit down lotus here
in front of me
Lay your hot palms
in my own two hands
Head to head, heart to heart
look me in the eye
and say out loud,
however softly:
"It wasn't my fault."

I give it back to you,
the anger and blessing mingling:
"No, it wasn't your fault,
it was never, ever your fault,
it was not your fault."

You were just a child
(It wasn't your fault)
You're a beautiful woman now
with so much good in you
to give the world
(No, it wasn't your fault)

They always try to say we did it
always place the blame on us
It wasn't my fault, either
I was just a little girl, too
another sweet spirit filled with joy
like you

It wasn't your fault
It wasn't my fault
No, it wasn't your fault,
it was never, ever my fault,
it was not your fault

Another sister's hands
join this circle of healing
She adds her voice
to the growing song:
"It wasn't your fault,
I love you,

Love yourself,
Forgive the awful nothing
that you did,
Love yourself,
Love yourself."

Look me, mirror, in the eye
and speak out loud and free:
It wasn't my fault
Goddamn the liars
It was not my fault
It was never, ever my fault
It was not my fault

It was not my fault
(sense the note of surprise)
It was not my fault
(hear the real conviction)
It wasn't my fault
(let the new-found knowledge sink through)

Now, say it with a smile
(I am laughing here with you,
helping to fan the sparkle inside)
It wasn't my fault
(she's up now, dancing,
pulling a chain of feet
to shout with her):

It wasn't our fault
It wasn't our fault
It wasn't your fault
It wasn't my fault

It wasn't our fault
It isn't our fault
It isn't our fault
It wasn't our fault . . .

(Chant this until you know
that it is true.)

I wrote this poem in the late summer and early fall of 1988. The words began coming to me soon after a session of our women's healing circle during which I had been gripped by something inside that rolled and screamed to be released from my body. I kept saying, over and over, "I want it to leave my body. Just leave my body. Just leave." This continued until Faith, the clairvoyant healer who led us, helped me to lie on the sidelines and calm down.

During the preceding year, I had begun to explore the monsters of my childhood in a series of "healing heart" poems, but none of my explorations had yielded concrete memories of specific sexual abuse—that is, nothing beyond the generalized kind of objectification, threat, and covert nastiness that is considered normal in this society. I had relived the sexual exploitation of my adolescence and young womanhood and had exorcised what I could in angry tears. So, I did not know exactly what was clamoring for release in me, what was being somehow propitiated through the writing of this poem, "No Fault." Nevertheless, I was, even then, as certain in my blood as I am now, after memories *have* surfaced, that I belong to the sisterhood of women who were sexually abused as little girls. It is for me as feminist therapists counsel: If you feel very strongly in the emotional-psychic body that you have been abused, you probably have been—even if there is nothing but this "gut" knowledge to support it.

At the time "No Fault" began to surface, the summer of 1988, I was back in Delaware preparing to move again, this time to California, because a wild chain of synchronistic events had led me to rescind one contract in order to accept another at the University of California, Santa Cruz. As I supervised the packing of my belongings, I composed lines of the poem in my head, all the while scrutinizing the men who were doing the work of packing—black men mostly, men who grinned and joked, who looked like members of the family and community I had known during my growing up days in the south. And I kidded and smiled in return, going through motions of friendly normalcy while gazing out from an inside rife with accusation: "Yeah, yeah, you guys act nice on the surface, but it's nice-acting men like you who abuse young girls. I bet at least one of the three of you has 'bothered' some niece or a girlfriend's daughter." And so it went inside my head. It was very strange, the sense of split, where the real reality was the scenes and the lines reverberating from within.

Not until another cycle of growth hit me in 1994 did the full force of what had begun with the "No Fault" poem blast through. In the interim, I had undergone numerous critical changes in my intimate relationships, my professional interests, my health and body, and my creative work. Continuing to search for a spiritual practice that really felt right, I had maintained the habit of extensively reading New Age materials, experimented with various forms of Buddhism, taken up study of the Alice Bailey teachings, and begun a daily, mentally focused meditation. Eventually, it all began to have the effect that comes from a good spiritual practice—that is, it brought to light, in a way that could be dealt with, the unattended areas of my being that needed attention.

Consequently, in 1995, I was propelled into a crisis of massive proportions, a stripping away of all the adjustments and adaptations that comprised my "self," the persona I was using to live in and deal with the world. The disintegration of this false self was a death so catastrophic that, by 1997, I was practically unable to find anyone inside that I could call "me" or who could say "I am." Some days I fell down to the floor and, both literally and figuratively, could not pick myself up. During those times, I kept remembering an old television movie that was, I believe, about El Cid, the eleventh-century Spanish soldier, or some other medieval hero.

During a war, El Cid is shot through the heart with an arrow the day before the decisive battle. He finds the pain unbearable, but he refuses to pull out the arrow because the instant loss of blood would mean his immediate death, and he feels it is essential for the morale of his troops that they see him up in front of them, leading them triumphantly into the fight. On the morning of the battle, El Cid is so near death that he has to be propped upright in his saddle with wooden poles. Like a cardboard cutout he moves forward upon his horse, facing the rising sun, the men thundering for miles around him. Already he is probably dead, just an illusion.

I felt like I was sending out a similarly dead, cardboard figure of myself every time I managed to go to work, while the real me lay as wasted as a beaten slave woman on the bedroom floor. To begin reconstructing myself, I had to reach all the way back into the murk and mire of my childhood. The first seven years were almost a total blank. I went into psychotherapy and began working with a gifted practitioner-healer who started guiding me through a reparenting program. I had been having fragmentary dreams of slugs and slime and preternaturally aware-but-silent, bare-bottomed, white-dressed little girls. Shortly, all these previously strange and inexplicable images made perfect sense as my mind's way of recording and playing back my early sexual abuse. I also realized that, during my nascent childhood years, I had been left alone and without care, either physically or psychically, or both.

Now, on the brink of significant spiritual maturation, I was being called upon to "grow up" and redeem my personality so that it could meet my expanding spiritual consciousness. One could not happen without the other. I suspect that many more people than the ones I know find that growing up spiritually requires—sooner or later—some form of "inner child" attention. When Alice Walker explained that meditation took her back to the way she had been as a child, crawling around eating sweet-smelling earth, knowing love and loving, she concluded, "So that's the paradise that's lost, that feeling of being at one with everyone and everything." Loss of childhood is loss of the spiritual kingdom within.

Still engaged in my recovery, I increasingly understand the work as soul process, knowing that—to the degree that I am able to feel and heal all the repressed hurt and shame—I will to that extent be able to express compassionately the connection that is the heart of love toward all my selves, brothers, and sisters. Spirituality catalyzes healing from political (society-related) ills and wounding, and this, in turn, enables greater spirituality.

The Spiritual Loners in a Corner

Masani Alexis DeVeaux talked about having it "laid upon" her to be "powerful" and says that she "came here with something" to express. Her statement suggests the hidden nature of much that constitutes our "growing up" and the fact that both visible factors and spiritual imperatives shape who we become. What is visible may appear to be non-heroic; however, spiritual power strongly pulses underneath the surface. Looking back over their childhoods, black woman after black woman who grew up to be fine and feisty told tales of how they had been quiet, different, and odd; loners who were "left" and isolated.

Early in our conversation, Sonia Sanchez surprised herself by saying that, of course, some people are born with the "veil" or caul over their face or body that indicates special, extrasensory abilities. More generally, "some people are born and, as they grow, they learn that they are spiritual. They know they are. No one's told them, no one's put a hand on them." When I asked her what she meant by the word "spiritual" in her remark, she replied by using as an illustration her own girlhood, which was marked by circumstances that developed her spiritual intuition and her reliance upon it.

When Sonia was one year old, her mother died giving birth to twins. Until she was six, Sonia and her older sister were raised by their grandmother, who then passed away. After her death, the girls were shunted from house to house of their extended family. Sonia began to stutter, a speech impediment she believes developed as a sort of "protective device." Her relatives regarded her as the "really odd and weird," "little one" who could not even "say a sentence, just go 'ah ah ah ah ah ah ah ah.'" Because her grandmother had taught her how to read by the time she was four years old, Sonia said people would simply "shove her someplace," saying things like "Give her a book, give her whatever, leave her." As a consequence, she spent a great deal of time alone. As Sonia recalls it now, "No one ever bothered me about anything, never consulted me about anything."

Labeled "strange," left to herself, Sonia "observed a lot." She would watch and try to figure out who was friendly, who was not. She also talked to herself—as well as to beings who talked back. This she never mentioned to anyone: "You pick up most certainly that if you're considered odd because of the way you speak, you know that if you say people talk to you, you would be relegated to an arena where you really can't come back. Yes, and I think that it happens a lot in children, because I think that children are very naturally open, real channels for spirits." Sonia would read, ask questions, close her eyes, and, lo, "there would be answers." Consequently, she "stayed sane." As a child, though, she did not see it as sanity. Looking back upon that time, she believes she was receiving companionship, perhaps from her deceased grandmother or mother.

In her aloneness, Namonyah Soipan took an even more active role. She used her intense creative energy to construct playmates who were so real that they assumed a dynamism of their own. "A loner as a child," she mainly played by herself, "read a lot," and "lived in a fantasy world." The characters she imagined were constantly around her, demanding that she act out their lives.

> I had to think for them, speak for them, and it would get really complicated, especially when they wanted to talk to each other. So I'm talking about some heavy-duty playing. This stuff started getting scary for me because I was losing a sense of reality. I would forget sometimes that they really didn't exist. And I would forget sometimes that I was really the main person in this scenario that I

had created. So I was always exhausted. My play always entailed a very sophisticated relationship between a man and a woman. And then somebody would be fighting over here [gesturing], so while I was concentrating on that interaction, then I would be pulled over here to deal with the animosity that was going on with this other particular group, and then something was going on somewhere else, so by the end of the day I was totally wiped out.

She had infused these characters with so much force that they existed independently of herself. Her mother got enough of a "peek" to become concerned. She thought that Namonyah was by herself too much, that her play was too intense, and that it was not the regular make-believe play of children with their dolls. Although Namonyah knew something more than "intense play" was occurring, she did not know exactly how to handle the situation. We discussed this in my interview:

> **Namonyah:** And I didn't know how to deal with it or how to seek help or whatever. Anyway, these characters took on so much life that they would invade my reality, even when I didn't want to deal with them, at school, when I was with other friends. They'd pull on me. I can't even believe I'm saying these things but I am anyway. So yeah, that's how it happened. Even as I look at that today, it may have something to do with spirituality in a way that I am not understanding, or spirits or energy or . . .

> **Akasha:** It's pretty clear to me that you had experience with the power of energy, and being in relationship with, even being the creator of it. And just like you were talk-

ing earlier about cracks between worlds—those are worlds and that's a place you bridged.

From her present perspective, Namonyah says about that early period of her life: "I may have been tapping into some spiritual energy or some spiritual awareness or reality that was beyond my scope, and certainly beyond [my parents']."

I agree with her assessment. Children, even very young ones, are capable of amazing things. Namonyah was accessing and manipulating in extremely powerful ways the creative energy of the universe, using it to fashion beings who were for her animated with life. At that early an age, she had instinctively discovered the mind's unbounded capacity to construct reality, and she was living routinely in the multidimensionality that is the true state of the universe, a multidimensionality that most adults prefer to suppress. Hers was the kind of creativity that is too often mislabeled madness.

Unusual only in degree and intensity, Sonia's and Namonyah's stories reveal how very open children are to receiving and using spiritual energy—and how this facility can be both a blessing and a challenge. Early years spent in the realms of the imaginary and the unseen begin a relationship to the spiritual world that is easily deepened and utilized later on—even if everything that is taught tends toward discrediting that realm. No doubt Namonyah's early experience with her playmates helped set her on her path as a seeker of religious and metaphysical truth.

Geraldine McIntosh's equally solitary childhood propelled her into rebellious directions, leading her to find and express spiritual anchoring through the mundane world. She grew up in Baltimore as an only girl among four brothers, in a family that taught her kin connection was essential (a very African concept) and freed her from "a lot of barriers." Her father impressed upon the boys that they were supposed to take care of her. Geraldine said, "We were never allowed to fight each other. For the most part my parents didn't really want us to socialize with a lot of children and we couldn't bring any kids in the house or to spend any nights, except if it was a cousin. My mother only socialized with her sisters. My brothers' best friends today are their cousins or somebody they knew in eighth grade who's been their friend for years and years."

Our real conversation about her girlhood ensued when I asked her to explain how she became the sort of person who, despite appearances to the contrary, lived a life that was, as she had pointed out, spiritually guided at its core. Because she believes—reminiscent of Sonia—that "some people are just really born into a lifestyle that is for some reason [spiritually] open," she began talking about herself as the Gemini child of Gemini parents, an astrological sign that she thinks predisposed them to the fluidity and introversion they exhibited. This duality, this "I do and I don't" personality governed her mother's stance on religion. Her mother sought *her* God in *her* home and believed that relationship with God was personal, and not a public show for Sundays. Further, because she did not have money to buy fancy clothes, she stressed that "you don't need no dress-ups to go to no church" and passed that on to her children.

> *Geraldine:* I had to beg my mother to let me be a Catholic. My mother didn't believe that you needed to go into

a building and dress up to praise God. She would tell me, "You can praise the Lord right here in this chair, if you're serious about doing that."

Akasha: Did she teach you how to praise the Lord sitting in that chair?

Geraldine: No. She would just always say that and by the time she said it, I would be in an ugly tizzy—just like her. She didn't really learn how to explain things to me calmly. I act so much like her. But I'm learning how to be calmer now as I grow. I know I'm untangling these thoughts. She didn't get the opportunity to untangle hers. She was still too busy struggling for survival. I know from being there what that feels like. The universe carried her through her life all right. So I knew where she was. No, she never explained, but she would not spend one dime for church clothes—and that's Easter or any other holiday. No, I didn't get no new shoes, and, no, I didn't . . .

Akasha: So, you did not go to church?

Geraldine: I did not go to church. Which was why I chose to be a Catholic because I really wanted to go, because all the children in the neighborhood belonged to some church. But I could be a Catholic and wear any clothes.

Geraldine believes that, as a consequence of her mother's attitudes, she did not erect a "boundary or barrier" around her values about how to be religious or about how clothes affect a person. She has decided that between her "mother and the universe, and just being a Gemini," she also learned how to operate from her heart: "When my head has to impose something on the top of my heart—and often it does for you to live in the world and just be safe—I have a problem." Although she grew up thinking that her mother's stringent treatment of her was cruel, she learned to appreciate its value. Therefore, when her mother fell ill, Geraldine was able to help her without anger getting in the way: "When it came time to be connected and be a child, be a part of that family, I had no major issues to resolve."

I asked her whether she felt like she had been given the opportunity to be a child. She replied: "Oh, not the kind of child that I wanted to be, no." When I suggested that her rearing was building confidence in her, she corrected me:

> I don't think I was building confidence. I just didn't put the non-confidence stuff there. So when I needed to draw on my inner strength for self-confidence, it wasn't clouded with lipstick. That stuff was easy to get rid of because I didn't get attached to it when I was a kid. A lot of things are just here on the outside of me. Even though I grew up with some childhood issues—and I haven't figured out what they all are—you know, around feeling isolated, feeling not a part of my mother, not feeling mother-daughterly—even though those were there, I still was blessed because I didn't get a lot of other negative external stuff. And somehow she conveyed that I must take care of myself.

These attitudes of trusting the self, relying upon the self, and looking within for guidance gave Geraldine an inner, ultimately spiritual, orientation. Therefore, regarding whatever information or experiences faced her, she was able to think independently and make correct life choices, listening to the voice of her own self-soul. Even today, she operates from what she herself knows her intent to be even though "what's gonna actualize and what people perceive in the world looks wrong as hell. But that doesn't stop me." She concludes,

> I had to work on getting rid of all that negative, self-degradation stuff I carry with me. You know, people say, "Girl, she done slipped again." But I would never stay there, because I really do have—not that I won't make mistakes—but I got this something that's real deep in me that says, "Oh no, I'm all right. I know I'm all right." I mean, you could just beat me, beat me, beat me and I'll know I'm all right.

This deeply held affirmation of essential self-worth is an indispensable spiritual resource. Michele Gibbs arrived at the same place of feeling "all right" with herself after a turbulent adolescent time. What she had to accept was a whole set of identities on the "left-hand" side. Michele was born, literally, left-handed, but her mother, who believed that this would further complicate her life, trained her out of it: "Every time I'd reach for something with my left, she would give it to me in my right hand. So being an Aries, I resisted for a long time, and I trained myself to be ambidextrous. Like at school, I can remember deliberately not only practicing reading signs backward, but writing with the left hand as well as the right. And I kind of kept that facility, but became for all intents and purposes right-handed." One day some years ago, while painting a mural in Grenada after having opened up to her repressed creativity, Michele looked up and, to her surprise, realized that she was painting with her left hand. Being left-handed is, for Michele, a metaphor for all the ways she has tried to develop her "other side"—non-rational thought, bisexuality as opposed to heterosexuality, going beyond the usual.

She has always known that her thought processes were not linear and that she had a photographic memory and an "associational process for apprehending the world." What has always stayed with her, what she has relied on to order her reality were the details that came out of "left field." Her parents, being communists and a black and white, mixed-race couple, always taught her, "Think for yourself." But her father took this even further:

> He would say things like, "When you read what's in a newspaper, start from the opposite conclusion and work your way back toward the middle and you might have a chance at arriving at the truth." So I never took what I was given literally, always felt I had to dig beneath it, get around it, look at it backwards, and then maybe I would come up with something. And so, that, I'm sure, freed me to pursue what was a natural bent.

After her family left Chicago and moved to Los Angeles, Michele's father died. She was fourteen years old, just beginning the third cycle of seven years that would take her into adulthood. As a result of these huge changes, she felt dislocated, "socially, culturally, physically, spiritually ripped." One day she walked around her neighborhood, staring up at the sky, talking to her father, communicating to him "the parts of why everything about me seemed to be different from everybody else around me":

And I remember coming to the conclusion that it wasn't just being left-handed, it wasn't just being a leftist, it wasn't just being bisexual because none of those are "just," and all of them fit into a piece. And I said, "Oh, it's everything," and as soon as I came to that point, it all became very positive because I said, "Oh, this is the way I am. It's not that this part of me is wrong and that part of me is wrong and the other part is wrong. It's that they're *all* right. They're all okay, and they're all different. But this is *all* me.

We exchanged a few words about this momentous happening:

Akasha: I got it, but. You could have looked at that whole list of your wrongness and come up with, "God, I'm all wrong," as opposed to saying it's *all* all right. So what do you see as being the thing that allowed you to take "all wrong" and come out on the other side with an "all right"?

Michele: It must have been something I got back from my father, I don't know. But I just remember, in that process, feeling an enormous sense of relief.

Akasha: So it must have been something that got . . .

Michele: Lifted, *um hmm.*

Akasha: Yes, to just be there and articulate all of that in the presence of whatever grace or message . . .

Michele: Or whim or caring.

Akasha: It came from him. And you definitely see it as something that came from him?

Michele: Oh, definitely, absolutely.

As with Sonia, this spiritual validation was crucial for her comfort and well-being.

Telling her story, Michele mentioned sneaking into off-limits sections of the library as a child. Hers was not a singular experience. In the intensity of our solitary growings-up, we women read books, all that the local school and public libraries offered, whatever we uncovered around our homes. They provided both entertainment and nourishment. I was so quiet that, my mother says, people thought she had only two, instead of three, children. I could usually be found somewhere with my "head in a book," devouring Bible stories rewritten for children, historical romances such as *Mandingo* and *The Saracen Blade,* other old hardbounds and discarded paperbacks that came from I-don't-know-where because we did not have the money to actually buy books.

Inveterate readers, we loner girls became the eager audience for literary works by African American women that began to tell true stories of our lives during the 1970s and '80s. Because that truth was about abuse and inadequacy as well as resourcefulness and survival, we gave our affirmation to books such as Toni Morrison's *The Bluest Eye,* Maya Angelou's *I Know Why the Caged Bird Sings,* and Alice Walker's *The Color Purple.* Even though the God in these texts appears to be, as the character Celie puts it, "trifling, forgitful and lowdown" about "poor colored women," he is not dead. In *The Bluest Eye* Pecola fervently prays to him for her blue eyes; in *The Color Purple* Celie herself had written him letters.

It is telling, however, that by the time we move from *The Bluest Eye* in 1970 to *The Color Purple* in 1982, the anthropomorphic white man of the Christian religion has been displaced by a female-centered spirituality. This new vision warmed those of us black women who were discovering new ways to be. What we saw was also of inestimable value in helping us to heal our wounded pasts and compromised presents. Childhood is a site that—unfortunately, or fortunately—generates the need for spirituality and spiritual healing, and simultaneously lays the foundation for that spirituality.

Working Out Soul Salvation

The lives of African American women are quite definitely a marvelous mix of hardship and grace, whim and caring. Without ignoring the stressful force, Toni Cade Bambara, in characteristic fashion, emphasized the positive aspects of her childhood. In fact, she traced everything she became back to her growing up years in 1940s radical Harlem and to her own early responsiveness to spiritual possibility.

At the time, she was the "little kid that doesn't go to bed," who was "everywhere," "very quiet, very discreet, reliable." As a "quick study," she could take minutes at a community meeting and also go anywhere she was sent to tell what had transpired at the gathering, shaping the narration to suit the interests and personality of her recipient, thereby gaining valuable training in group dynamics and analysis. On her own, Toni hung out in the street with her skates. If there was a meeting of people whom she liked—"warrior types"—then she would attend the meeting. Even as a young girl, eight or nine years old, she was, as she put it, "drawn to fire." Like Michele, she was born under the astrological sign of Aries, one of the three fire signs.

In that Harlem setting, the only point of view Toni knew was a black one. And the only reason she went to school was "to hassle white people." Real learning took place at Speaker's Corner, and at the Marcus Garvey Liberation Bookstore. In the basement of the bookstore, where children were not allowed, were the special black gnostic books. Sometimes little study groups met down there. At those times she could take off her skates, go sit on the stairs, and listen—or catch her breath before going on to the next errand. At the same time as she was eavesdropping on the metaphysical study groups, from the women of the Sanctified and Pentecostal churches Toni heard Christianity explicated in a black, radical way—related to issues of the day such as consumer education and economic co-ops. Thus she was imbibing a sense of spirituality as both metaphysics-religion and world activism—a hallmark of her later work and of a great deal of African American spirituality.

Another of Toni's stopping places was the steps of the black Schomburg library. Because children were also prohibited there, since they might have "dirty, sticky hands and chewing gum," she remained on the steps or leaned on the posts and accosted people. She would "yank on their dress," "yank on their pants leg," and, "fresh like," ask them, "So, what do you know?" John Henrik Clarke, the historian, sat down and told her some things. Camilla Williams, the operatic singer, talked to her about music and discipline and the pursuit of excellence. At this point, the "whole question of spirit and that realm below the sensible world" came in:

I began to notice that most people, whether they were artistic, intellectual, political, whatever—by way of explaining their process, their person, their question, their mission—invariably had to resort to talking about either God or spirits or intuition or a dream or something like that. And in our house we did not. This was not the frame of reference. So I began to be interested in exactly that frame of reference, as well as all others. But especially that frame of reference because I heard so few echoes and confirmations of it at home—which is not to say my mom and dad did not listen to Wings Over Jordan and go to church. But there was something else, and they were not into that.

In homes and on the streets, the Communist party organizers (who were the most visible) were very scientific. When they got to that point of deep explanation, Toni says, they would either stop or "go into some Marxist dialectic." She would continue to press them, "Well, if it's a true dialectic, where's the spirit, or where do ideas come from?"

Akasha: And you were asking that like that?

Toni: Maybe not like that, but that's what I was after because I wanted to hear that thing again. I wanted to hear people hit that note again. For example, when Camilla Williams would talk about being visited (that's how she said it) by the spirit of music, when she would say it, she would straighten up and glow, and she'd give me a little trill [sound] (she was always practicing). Or when J. A. Rogers or someone like that explained why they do what they do, why it's important, why black people have to know, and that Beethoven had a black grandmother, which seemed foolish to me. I mean, it did seem silly: grown man trying to pull out black genes. My position was always, "Well, what was Beethoven's position on slavery? If you can't tell me that, I don't care who his grandma was."

Yet, despite whatever reservations she may have brought to the particular enterprises of these individuals who attracted her, Toni respected and learned from them:

So, when J. A. Rogers would get all het up about his mission and why it was important, because I guess I was asking exasperating questions, he would finally hit on something like, "The mission of African peoples in the world. . . ." He'd get all metaphysical and something. He would get tall and his shoulders would broaden and chin would sharpen and he would be trembling, kind of. So I figured, whatever this thing is, whatever this spirit level is, is very heavy and it does something to your body. It straightens it up, it broadens it out, expands your lungs, and so it might be something I want to know more about.

Thus Toni heard the high note of spirit and saw its workings in a manner that indelibly impressed her. She declares that later—whether in a dream workshop, or taking a meditation class, or celebrating the equinoxes, or doing group rituals—"whatever it is I seem to know in those moments, I can always trace the inspirational beginnings to that period of growing up in Harlem, running around on skates."

Perhaps her recognition of that spirit sound, that metaphysical reality emanated from her own direct knowledge. Toni has always been available to spirit. As did so many of the women with whom I spoke, she linked this fact to having grown up in a household that threw her back upon her own resources:

> We moved around a lot. There was a lot of terror in the family; there was a lot of confusion in the family. My mother was an orphan, my father was a runaway. They did not know what they were doing. I had a brother who came into the world as a child prodigy and then began to fade. So in that household was no sense of any consistency, no sense of any standards, no sense of definitions, no sense of any core. So it was necessary for me to find some anchor, some stabilizer. And one of the things I found—I found many—but one of the things I found was a notebook. Keep a notebook; keep track of yourself. Things would get lost. Promises got lost. Dreams got lost. People's shoes got lost, whatever. So I felt if I could just have a lost and found, which was this little notebook, that maybe I could get through this traumatic period.

In that journal, when she was six-and-a-half years old, Toni recorded her first conscious brush with spirit lives. On V-J Day in August 1945, while vacationing with her family, Toni was lying facedown in high grass near a dairy in Northfield, Vermont. Smelling the aromas and "having a conscious thought of myself in the world," she mused: "Gee, I'm a person; I exist; I have a thought in my head. I'm in the world. What a marvelous thing." At that exact moment, the bells and alarms signaling the armistice began to sound, and people started screaming, jumping up and down, carrying on. Toni wonders if this is "what the Christians call Judgment Day," and then she gets scared because she spies white people running around drunk. Even though there is nothing in her particular experience to draw on, her "race memory" tells her that "this can be a dangerous situation." Spinning out the story as we talked, she continued:

> And then I feel coming up behind me on both sides a visitation, and this is not new, but it's new, too, because it usually happens at night. Evidently those kinds of visits must have been usually in the night when I'm sleeping and I'm aware through an aroma—usually linseed oil, which is my mother's mother—or cinnamon, which is this other woman—or I don't know what that other aroma was, a kind of curry smell, which are these two Native American guys. No, this was a visitation in daylight in the middle of all this noise, and they were coming up around me and they were going to lean down and tell me something.

And as they leaned down, Toni thought, "I have choices. I can be spooked, I can go crazy and scream like everybody else, I can listen quietly and hear what they have to say." Just as they were about to speak, she closed her eyes, and "that rational thing," "that critic kicks in" and tells her, "There ain't nobody there. And if you open your eyes and look and see nobody there, this'll be over, this sequence will be over. Do you want it over?" Simultaneously, another part of her said, "You know nobody's there, and if you turn around and look and there actually *is* somebody there, what are you going to do about that: go crazy or what?":

So, I'm so busy, there's all this noise going on inside me, which is not so much these thoughts I have just articulated, but whatever sensations are closest to it. And that's so noisy that I don't hear [what the visitors speak]. And I say, "Oh damn," or whatever a little kid says, six years old. But I write this in my diary, in my log, and I write (I was looking at this not long ago), I write, "When next they come, I will be calm and I will be quiet."

This early experience became a reference point for her that she describes in this way:

You know that feeling you have sometimes when you're walking along minding your business—you ain't doing nothing particular, kind of in neutral, on automatic pilot? And all of a sudden you get this wave of affirmation, "YES, YES! Right! Ah, Ah!" And if you allow for one minute that rational critic to kick in and say, "Yes what? Yeah right? What are you talking about?" the whole thing will dissipate, and then you'll walk down the stairs feeling a little foolish. Thereafter those periods for me of "YES! YES!" were sometimes accompanied by this sensation of the guardians on either side.

With Geraldine's "I'm all right," Michele's "I'm all all right"—graced by her dead father, and Toni's "Yes, Yes" wave of affirmation between her spirit guides, we can see how, out of the crucible of trying early beginnings, so many African American women have forged strength and possibility. And we have done so under the aegis of heaven, so to speak, encompassed and often protected within the scheme of divinity. It seems that, "from the earliest rocking of our cradle," we all have been set up for what it is we are ultimately to become and achieve. This observation leads us to consider the teachings that say that our souls/spirits choose or manufacture for us the experiences we need in order to continue with the work of evolution. This observation also prompts us to recall what author A. A. Milne's Christopher Robin tries to impress upon his bear friend, Winnie the Pooh: "Remember, you are braver than you believe, stronger than you seem, and smarter than you think." His words are a wonderful little formula—encompassing all three aspects of our personal selves: strong bodies, brave emotions, smart minds, with the accurate pun that how we rationally think is only the least part of our smartness.

When Christopher Robin says "Remember," the word *remember* carries even greater meaning. Ultimately, what we are fighting to remember, to put back together, is our true and powerful spiritual identity, the knowledge that was relinquished when we incarnated into these material body-minds. It is this real, all brave-strong-smart self that we want to wake up to (to be like the Buddha who, when asked whether he was a man, simply replied, "I am awake"). The poem "Ode: Intimations of Immortality from Recollections of Early Childhood," by the English Romantic poet, William Wordsworth, which some of us were exposed to in high school or college—but often without this enlightening explanation—expresses the idea: "Our birth is but a sleep and a forgetting: / The Soul that rises with us, our life's Star, / Hath had elsewhere its setting." Wordsworth says that we are born into this earthly realm "trailing clouds of glory."

When we first enter existence in the physical world, we know that we are immortal spirit, but as we adapt ourselves to the mundane order, we forget—and have to spend our lifetime attempting to remember as much about our spiritual origins as we can. However, as young ones, we are closer to the divine "glory," and it serves us well. Geraldine said, sadly, that we may not have enjoyed the childhoods we would have wanted. However, from a higher perspective, they were the perfect ones; they were the ones our spirits required for growth and ultimate fulfillment. We can make this spiritual acknowledgment even as we actively deplore and resist the abuses of spirit that take form as sexual exploitation, emotional abandonment, miseducation, systematic poverty, racial oppression, discrimination based on personal differences, and so on. Seeing how we grow up—appearances notwithstanding—as spiritually perfect is an especially heartening perspective for African American women and other women of color. Because of the concatenation of racist and sexist forces—institutional, external, and internalized—that play through our existences, we are often dealt complicated or trying lives.

Usually, abused children are regarded as victims. We are, and we are not. Let me begin by describing the way in which we *are*. Fundamentally, abuse perpetrated upon children is a direct violation of their spirituality because it fails utterly to recognize and validate the divine and loving self that they intuit they are and have the potential to be, and often still try to be even in the face of the most horrible crimes against them. Psychologically, abuse of a child—especially if it is sexual—so objectifies the child that it can nearly obliterate the child's sense of self, including the spiritual self. If the abuse is incestuous, there is added betrayal, for, as has been stressed by insightful therapists, parents and parental figures are a child's first "god." If the abuser also harms with words, those words coming from a larger authority figure carry the all-knowing, all-controlling force of divine fiat, even more so when the abuser is a religious figure, someone like the deacon in my poem, "No Fault." These forms of abuse all directly interfere with the child's developing spirituality.

So, understanding how sexual abuse victimizes children is easy and straightforward. It is not as simple, however, to grasp how children in these circumstances are not victims. It is important to understand that when I suggest it is possible for them not to be considered victims, I am by no means preparing to mount the argument that—in some perverse psychological manner— they collude in or "ask for" what they get. That is not the direction in which I am heading. What I *do* want to explain is my intuition that the process of living through and surviving childhood sexual abuse can foster redemption on two interconnected levels—the worldly and the spiritual. As I use the word here, *redemption* is what occurs when something is transformed ("saved") into its best and highest state by virtue of necessary, inevitable, and/or graceful action. And that "something" that can be redeemed or transformed in the case of sexual abuse is the abhorrent act of the abuser and its consequences. Let me be clear: by examining sexual abuse from this broader and more unusual spiritual perspective, I am not excusing or sanctioning any form of abuse. Although it can be understood in a metaphysical, transcendent way that helps us come to terms with its existence in the world, abuse is still a travesty of human and spiritual rights that must be vigorously combated at every level.

A personal story will help to illustrate and anchor this concept of transformative redemption that can come from an experience of trauma. It is the story of one of the "mildest" incidents of sexual abuse (if any sexual abuse could be considered "mild") that I experienced while growing up. When I was about ten years old, Mr. Glover, the man next door who was also our landlord, came up to me in the driveway near the back of his house. He pinched my budding breasts, then gave me a weird, shitty grin and a fifty-cent piece and told me not to tell anybody. Wronged and upset, I rushed through our kitchen door and told my mother. What I remember of her reaction is that she said she would tell my father when he came home. I don't know what—if anything—ever happened after this.

When Mr. Glover pinched my breast, he hurt me physically, on a cellular level. At the same time, he greatly disturbed my emotional body—a disturbance which agitated ripples of worthlessness and shame. His actions threw terrible confusion into my mind: How could I begin to make sense of what he had done? Whether I wanted to or not, I had to deal with this abuse. As grace or karma or whatever would have it, I was able to respond in an oppositional way. I lived through his actions intact enough as a person to run and tell my mother, and this speaking out was the initial blow in my attempt at fighting back. It has taken years to debunk the shame and constriction that took hold that day and to achieve some steady sense of understanding. I have done so by assiduously repairing the damage to myself and by strenuous opposition to everything that Mr. Glover and violations like his represent.

Through the undoing of what Mr. Glover did to me, I have learned and grown, and I have been empowered. In the process, I have helped others to achieve the same by sharing my story, giving advice and comfort, and so on. I even see this particular incident as relating to the work of education and spirituality that I have assumed as my purpose in the world. Thus, a terrible act—and its consequences—have thereby been redeemed. This present telling of the story is the latest—and perhaps final—place to which I have taken the transformative possibilities of this event.

My response to what happened to me illustrates one way that sexual abuse can be redeemed. Dealing with abuse, and struggling against it at the worldly level is a critical means via which redemption transpires on *both* worldly and spiritual levels. Reparenting, building, or rebuilding the self pushes forward the motion of spiritual redemption by breaking cycles of violence and victimization. The force of a "No!" shouted by a girl or woman, along with her decision to heal, calls forth the power of light to counteract and to transform. She begins to change the situation; she begins to reclaim and redeem herself. In this role, she is, in a sense, remembering who she truly is and where she came from, taking on the work that is soul choice, or metaphysical being, or infinite and unknowable process. In either case, it is holistic and holy work.

However, my story could have turned out differently. I could have been crushed, I could have stayed mired in the worthlessness and shame of the abuse, I could have become a child molester. As tragic as any of these other outcomes may be, they would still have played their part in the ultimate redemptive process. Let me explain, using a kind of metaphysical framework.

The first idea to be considered is that practically all of us on this Earth have almost totally forgotten our spiritual origins, and all of us, all the time, are busy living our lives, actively engaging in the experiences that will return us to that forgotten state of pure spirit from which we came. As human beings, having experience is the only way that we gradually learn and/or remember who we really, essentially are. Thus, going back to our spiritual origins means going *through* the material (matter), a truism reminiscent of our flip saying about difficulties: the only way out of them is through them.

If one imagines a spirit-matter continuum with spirit at the top and matter at the bottom, then the journey proceeds from that high, topmost place all the way through to the lowest place before it reverses itself, ultimately completing what has been from the very beginning a return trip home. Along the way, everything touched by the energy of spirit is pushed to its furthest growth and potential—wherever it is on its own spirit-matter path. This process of the eventual spiritualization of matter is, in the truest sense, redemption. Like medieval alchemy, the process transmutes something from one state into another state more consonant with its best nature and possibilities—into something with enhanced value and worth. This redemptive process tends toward the positive even when that does not appear to be the case. Whatever or whoever embarks on this journey is always on the eventual way up even when headed down. And this process is at work at every level, in each little experience or relationship, each lifetime.

What this means—and this is the difficult part—is that everything we do, every experience we have is, from this large, metaphysical, spiritual perspective, redemptive. Abuse magnifies what happens during this process of the ultimate spiritualization of matter because it slams the abused person into feeling worthless and not like a child of God (Spirit). Thus, the work of struggling back to the knowledge of self as a spiritual child, so to speak, highlights in a dramatic way what is going on all the time, for all of us, in each and every situation (since all experience is redemptive). Also, in highly charged and freighted situations, when much is at stake, we are often being confronted with the issues that are most critical for our growth. Being able to meet them forthrightly and handle them so that as much light as possible is invoked through our active engagement hastens the redemption—although, slowly or faster, it inevitably occurs.

If I had done nothing but "take" the abuse of Mr. Glover—or had been utterly devastated by it—my presence in that situation would still have served redemptive purposes—that is, I would nevertheless have functioned as the means by which material denseness, through active experience, furthered its progress toward spiritual being and light. That which is spiritual (the drive or movement toward fulfilled good, embodied in me as a developing child) passed through that which is the physical at its grossest (the pull into the denseness of materiality that has lost touch with its spiritual origins, embodied in Mr. Glover, the violator). On that journey, that which is spiritual enhanced its own spirituality and, simultaneously, assisted in the overall process of spiritualization that engages every being and every entity on this planet (including the violator).

Undergoing experience, being touched by the light and energy of operative spirit and spiritualization, Mr. Glover may have responded, too, in more than one way. He may—almost immediately, or after a talk with my father—realized his great wrong and repented, never to transgress again, thereby making an upward move with respect to this particular issue and episode of his life. Or he could have sunk deeper into his perfidy. Sometimes, whatever needs transforming is driven by the touch of spirit into even darker denseness before it makes the crucial turn toward light, toward any glimmer of perception of its goodness and divinity, what Buddhists would call "true Buddha nature." Although eventually, somewhere along the trajectory, either later in the lifetime I knew him or in some subsequent time or incarnation, Mr. Glover would have to see the light, I have no way of knowing when or if this has occurred. What I do know is that the sad encounter between us when I was ten was an episode in both of our spiritual journeys.

So, again, I am not talking about accepting wrong or wrongdoing. Believing that all life—including ourselves and our actions—will inevitably become sacred and whole does not give us license to behave in a horrible or life-negating fashion. Nor does this let us off the spiritual hook. Because we ourselves are also spirit, on that hook, we are perpetually swinging. We must choose right and light, we must wake up to our own goodness and the goodness of others—otherwise, the reason why we and this universe exist will not be fulfilled. Reaching the point of manifested fulfillment and redemption requires our participation. Understanding this, it makes much more sense to begin making transformative choices sooner rather than later. This is infinitely better and more in keeping with the life force within us than is retarding the process by requiring spirit to exert repeated energy and ever-greater pressure to get us to do the right thing.

Wrong and wrongdoing, wherever they exist, rightfully must be battled by every means within our power, as imperatively as the work of healing the abused child is embraced. What I have strained to communicate throughout this discussion is a higher and wider understanding of abuse, one that reaches to its esoteric, or underlying, significance. From this perspective, we can begin to view such travesties in a light beyond personal grief and outrage—by, for example, coming to terms with the existence of evil as a temporary stage in the unfolding of a bigger and better plan. Being able to think in this way may have helped me as I was struggling through the writing of "No Fault," baffled and angry, asking out loud, "What kind of bastard would have done something so awful to a precious baby girl?"

Viewing abuse as a difficult aspect of the ultimate spiritualization of the material world places it in a larger perspective that shifts the balance of power from abuse and victimization to the inexorable movement toward wholeness, that seemingly slow blunder toward the day when all of us will be sufficiently in touch with our soul-spirit-god selves not to behave in contrary ways. This spiritual perspective, finally, makes those of us who hardly and, especially, consciously participate in that movement *not victims but redeemers,* not even survivors but redeemers, turning what has been done to us and what we are doing to evolutionary account. As we fight, heal, endure, and transform, as we tell our stories and do our work, we act in that redemptive process and power.

In my discussion of spirituality and healing, I have focused on abuse in order to clarify the meaning of redemption. Let me now briefly widen the view to include the spiritual "work" of children in general. As the childhood accounts of individuals in this chapter illustrate, children are very busy at much more than play. They have experiences that teach them about the spiritual world. They spend time being young, spiritually oriented people—exploring solitude, becoming conversant with the inner self, touching their higher minds and guiding intuition. And they attract the things that lay the foundation for their later life endeavors, orienting to specific paths and spiritual destinations. Beyond all this, children serve a larger, collective—and likewise redemptive—purpose. Each generation takes what has been left to them, the material of their civilization, and, by the force of spirit pulsing in them, seeks to bring that to a higher level. Everyone senses this about the role of the next generation, and somehow understands that it pulls humankind further along the evolutionary scale. Whatever is wrong, whatever has not been done, there is usually hope that the oncoming generation may make it right.

"As below, so above." If we take what has emerged from examining our "little" lives and think in these terms about the larger life of our society, of the world and the universe, we can be likewise encouraged. What flowered around 1980 was the beginning of a very significant cycle of growth. As a whole, humanity is trying to grow up and spiritually heal. The cataclysmic events we call World War I and World War II were illnesses on a physical level that ravaged countries, cities, buildings, houses, and land. By comparison, the current world crisis hinges on especially rich and/or developed countries and their willingness to release their emotional attachment to material wealth so that all the world's people are properly nurtured and fed and the planet can be saved from ecological destruction. Imagine the kind of upheaval analogous to the wars that would force us to make that choice. A scary thought. Some futurists say a worldwide crash of the stock markets and financial system would usher in a much-needed redistribution of our natural and monetary resources.

I do not know. But I do believe that the crisis-forged qualities of deep caring and compassion requisite to the health and well-being of the individual self are the same ones required for our body politic. In fact, hope emerges when we realize that individual healing and growth (happening now at an accelerated pace) contribute to the wholeness of the group, moving us all that much further in the right direction. As one-by-one we re-birth and re-grow as part of our spiritual maturation, we contribute to that potential wholeness for our larger aggregates—partners, families, work and friendship circles (which are often our soul/spiritual groups), communities, the nation, the world, and universe.

This redemptive process is modeled by the African American women whose lives are assembled in this book. Every time Toni Cade Bambara exhorted all of us, as human beings, to think and behave better than we have been programmed to by the system and to "simply slip into the power, into the powerful power hanging unrecognized in the back-hall closet," she was pushing her grown-up version of the formula A. A. Milne provided his characters: Yes, we are, in essence, braver than we believe, stronger than we seem, and smarter than we think.

≈6≈

SPIRITUAL, BLACK, AND FEMALE:
CARRYING POWER INTO THE TWENTY-FIRST CENTURY

Now is a power time for women. At the end of my interview with Toni Cade Bambara, she disclosed that "the adepts"—and not just female ones who might be accused of self-promotion— were saying that from 1981 until the first decade or so of the twenty-first century, women would be leading in spirituality. Lucille Clifton stated the very same thing: "You know, I was told that the women were going to be carrying the spiritual power for a while. Somebody who's not alive told me that. I went for it." Others have made similar statements, sometimes with and sometimes without the kind of documentation from higher, suprahuman sources that Toni and Lucille provide.

Speaking from a more racially specific perspective, Alice Walker asserted that African American women have deployed supernatural power because "this is the one thing the slave masters couldn't steal. They can take your body, but not your soul. They couldn't kill the spirit." And Dolores Kendrick ventured that, as we black people "dig deeper into our roots, it's inevitable that we tap that vein that we now call the other, psychic self. I think that's what is happening, and for some reason, it's been the black women doing it."

African American women are indeed "doing it"—are still being spiritual carriers in a predominantly white, patriarchal society. Not surprisingly, however, in this world where gender discrimination rules, our spiritual status meets with both success and opposition, as was evident when the renaissance of black women's literature of the late 1970s and early '80s encountered misreadings and hostility. Nevertheless, among ourselves, black women continue to gather and celebrate in spirit-driven ways, as evidenced, for instance, by the African American Women on Tour conference series, now commemorating its tenth anniversary. In public media such as television and film, black women are playing a strong role in conveying spiritual themes and material. To look at these media phenomena extends our exploration of this new spirituality into arenas that are equally as important as lived experience and books.

On her unprecedented, influential daytime television talk show, Oprah Winfrey puts her prestige behind the idea that therapeutic spiritual techniques and methods as developed by experts such as Phil McGraw, Iyanla Vanzant, and Gary Zukav can be brought to mass audiences of people in order to help them positively change their lives. In film, black women filmmakers are unique in including personal altars in their cinematic vision and originally depicting diverse African American spiritual practices. Kasi Lemmons's 1997 independent film, *Eve's Bayou*, is a glowing example of this achievement, although it was passed over by the NAACP Image Awards, with recognition given instead to the male-made and commercial *Soul Food,* which was a far more superficial film.

Finally, among women in general, Hillary Rodham Clinton—during her tenure as first lady—revealed a seeming openness to New Age understandings that was, unfortunately, subverted by the weighty institutional apparatus surrounding her. From the movie theater to the White House, entrenched left-brain forces slow down the onrush of twenty-first century, spiritually-progressive female energy—even as this energy persists in manifesting itself.

Paying Homage to the Spirit and the Blood

From the 1980s to the 1990s, the collective spiritual consciousness of black women continued to grow, both keeping pace with and contributing to the burgeoning New Age. One nationwide example of black female activity organized around, grounded in, or impelled by spiritual consciousness is the African American Women on Tour conference series, which began under the direction of San Diego-based Maria Carothers. Each year the three-day conference takes place in California cities and travels east to locales such as Washington, D.C., New Orleans, Chicago, and New York City. A specific theme addresses the ultimate empowerment of black women who convene in large numbers to experience highly charged workshops, the words of inspirational keynote speakers, and joyful social mingling. Carothers's 1993 program letter gave the participants the following assurance:

> Trust that when we leave this hotel on Sunday, we'll all be transformed. The spirit—that higher presence—

will have moved us many times over, and we will have cultivated sister friendships to cherish a lifetime. The important thing is to keep our minds and hearts open and free; free to be cleansed and nourished with the many positive images of sisters "thinking their thoughts" and "doing their do."

That year the conference headliners were Terry McMillan, whose novel, *Waiting to Exhale,* was a recent sensation; Attallah Shabazz, who spoke about the need to include the youth; Julianne Malveaux, addressing economic self-sufficiency; and Iyanla Vanzant, a conference mainstay, who called upon the healing and assistance of spirit throughout daily life, drawing on her own elevation from welfare recipient in an abusive relationship to educated author, speaker, and priestess.

Many small workshops, limited in attendance to between fifteen and twenty, took participants to deeply emotional, culturally resonant places, regardless of their topic. One workshop, entitled "Calling Forth the Inner Healer," incorporated African ritual, smudging, a gentle beating of the drum, the passing of candles, and a climactic gazing into mirrors. Prominent authors were always invited to the conferences, showing the close linkage that exists between black women writers and the progressive consciousness of black women as a whole. Other years were highlighted by the appearance of Alice Walker, Bebe Moore Campbell, and Maya Angelou.

When I asked one of the attendees what she would say about how large a role spirituality played in the conferences, whether explicit or not, she replied: "I would say it is kind of like being in church, in a black women's church—drawing collective strength from the common stories—people shouting amen and waving their napkins, laughing and crying. There's a sense of connection that's invisible, this energy you don't have to talk about." Never mind that the emphasis on spirituality places these conferences in a general category with the innumerable such workshops, seminars, and meetings that are taking place these days. Never mind that the actual spiritual traditions incorporated are not all specifically African-derived. Never mind, even, that there may be nothing uniquely African American female about needing empowerment.

While I say "never mind" in speaking of these characteristics, what I really want to communicate is that in impetus and motivation, content, tone, and feeling, these gatherings are richly and resonantly black. Both poles of the compass are needed to guide us to a true understanding of African American women's spirituality at the turn of this important century—that is, the way it partakes of ancient wisdom and New Age elements while remaining historically and racially grounded. Despite the smudging and the mirrors, the conference participants felt as if they were in "a black women's church" and waved their napkins as though they held "Negro" funeral home fans decorated with the face of Jesus.

African American Women on Tour is important because it has helped large numbers of black women tap into, strengthen, and use the power of their spiritual will. In 2001, the Tour will celebrate its tenth anniversary with meetings between May and September in St. Kitts and Nevis, West Indies; Atlanta, Georgia; and Los Angeles, California (three sites instead of the usual six). Now headed by executive producer Maria Denise Dowd, the conference has picked up very visible sponsorship from corporations such as ExxonMobil, Sprint, Bank of America, Nabisco, American

Airlines, Hanes, Merck, and Time Warner. The current statement of purpose notes that the "over 150 dynamic workshops on career development, financial management, family relations, health, business development, and Rites of Passage programs" are "all designed to support your personal career and economic advancement." In keeping with this goal, there are fewer writers who keynote and more motivational experts. "Economic, intellectual, and spiritual development" are hailed as the means by which African American women can enhance their quality of life.

Obviously, activities related to spirituality and spiritual development have become more mainstream and more commercial. In this atmosphere, precisely what "spiritual" means may be harder to discern. However, I view the continued evocation of spirit and spirituality as positive, a good sign indicative of our evolutionary sense as human beings that we are comprised of higher, transpersonal aspects that motivate and aid us and that call for our focused attention and nurturing. Invoking spirit also seems to acknowledge a larger, divine order to which we are tied in fundamental and beneficent ways.

When Toni Cade Bambara and Lucille Clifton declare that women will be carrying spiritual power into the twenty-first century, they are saying, I believe, that women will, as a group, be more attuned than men, as a group, to the revolutionary possibilities inherent in spirit connection, and they will be more instrumental in accessing, manifesting, and spreading this energy. I further believe that African American women, specifically, have a crucial role to play in this transmission of spiritual consciousness, a role clearly seen first in the rise of supernatural and esoteric content in their literature during the 1980s. This mission, if you will, is still apparent in the awareness with which progressive

African American women are living their lives and is visible, on a grand, individual scale, in the phenomenon of Oprah Winfrey and her enormously popular daytime television talk show.

Oprah has achieved iconic status, and her name is a household word. Beginning her life as an abandoned and maltreated little girl on a pig farm in Mississippi, she has pulled herself through childhood sexual abuse, teen pregnancy, and an uncertain initial career to become one of the most powerful women in the United States, with a reported net worth of $725 million. Her television program is viewed by an estimated 22 million people in the United States every week. It has been the number one talk show for fourteen consecutive seasons since its debut in 1986. From this influential position, Oprah has increasingly focused on spiritual issues and self-help information, totally reformatting the program in 1998 as "change your life television."

For that 1998–99 season, she launched a series of programs under the rubric, "Remembering Your Spirit," which featured a lineup of leading New Age spiritual experts. Guests included John Gray, author of *Men Are from Mars, Women Are From Venus*, on removing the emotional blocks hindering personal success and achieving "your soul's desire"; Dr. Cherie Carter-Scott explaining the "Rules for Being Human"; Caroline Myss, author and medical intuitive, on how healing of the spirit can lead to bodily healing; Sarah Ban Breathnach on how to acquire a more healthy self-love.

Mark Bryan, co-collaborator with Julia Cameron on wealth and creativity enhancement, appeared on a show about absent fathers, a topic resonant for many white people these days as they come to terms with male parents who were emotionally unavailable to them because of work, alcohol, or some other preoccupation or illness. It is perhaps even more relevant for African Americans whose legacy of absent fathers harks far back to enforced separation during slavery and, more recently, to welfare guidelines that mandated no men be in the house. "Life strategist" Dr. Phil McGraw helped guests to change their lives before the year 2000. He has since become a program regular, appearing every Tuesday for "Dr. Phil's Day." All of these featured experts are white—showing, still again, how rare it is for New Age spiritual expression by people of color to gain visibility in this predominantly white, money-driven society.

One exception has been Iyanla Vanzant, black female "empowerment specialist, spiritual life counselor, and ordained minister," as her book jackets describe her. As part of Oprah's "Remembering Your Spirit" series, Iyanla—like two or three other guests—has appeared a number of times. She has been particularly effective with audiences of single women. On the January 4, 1999 show that presented Iyanla's life story, Oprah mentioned that her appearances had generated the heaviest volume of mail.

What spiritual technologists like Iyanla do, especially in a forum such as *Oprah*, is what I term "applied spirituality," by which I mean that ancient wisdom and metaphysical, esoteric, and spiritual teachings are not specifically articulated in any intellectually demanding fashion, but that these truths underlie ideas and techniques that are used to help large numbers of people in very practical ways. The two times that I saw Iyanla, she absolutely did not allow studio guests to name-call individuals they were involved with by using appellations such as "jerk": He's not a jerk, she interdicted, but a "child of God" who is presenting you with a "divine opportunity" for necessary experience. Of course, everyone laughed—and cried—because the shift in consciousness she was facilitating is profound, and profoundly true.

Iyanla's re-framing directs attention away from the "jerky" ways of the lower personality and toward the recognition of our transpersonal spiritual selves, an identity infinitely more reliable and promising, one that, if we manage to hold onto it, will ultimately guide us aright. Her re-framing also affirms the always everywhere holographic matrix that binds and interconnects us in a divine and dynamic system of constant change and growth. Of course, Iyanla did not give a lecture about any of this. She simply led the woman who was miserable about her boyfriend or complaining about her boss to lift to the higher consciousness through a reprogramming of thought via language.

Another of her techniques was an acceptance-and-willingness exercise where one completes the following statements: "Today, I accept that I have experienced . . ." and "Today, I am willing to . . ." This similarly deep move places some objective distance between the personality who lives in the human world and suffers and the spiritualized consciousness that can calmly view these happenings, an attitude of detachment that teachers in many traditions tell us is the first step toward self-control and transmutation. Meditation confers such detachment, but some members of the audience writing down this formula in their "Homework for the Soul" notebooks may not have been regular meditators. Finally, the "willingness" affirmation calls into action the spiritual will—willpower being the first attribute of divinity, which, operating in a triple whole with love and intelligence, makes it possible for us to "get moving" on our paths.

In featuring these "Remembering Your Spirit" topics, Oprah acts out of her own considerable spiritual consciousness, which she—in inimitable Oprah fashion—in turn put on display, going where Iyanla and the other experts directed, but also quoting her own favorite verses from the biblical book of Psalms. Also, as sophisticated as Iyanla's knowledge is regarding spiritual energy and laws of the universe, she refers, quite simply, to "God" as the source of her blessings and well-being, again evidencing the blending of traditional and New Age elements.

Essentially, Oprah has been making innovative ideas and healing modes available to huge numbers of people who may otherwise not have paid attention to them. She puts her prestige and power behind this material, distributing it on daytime television (even if in a stepped-down and sometimes slightly "dramatic" way). I know that many individuals, including myself, could never imagine opening up our most private selves for consumption by a mass television audience—revealing painful intimacies, crying, being used as willing therapeutic examples. But I also know that just as many of us are frequently drawn into what we witness, our reservations notwithstanding.

For instance, on the November 21, 2000, program—one of Dr. Phil's days, he led the audience in a "relationship rescue workshop," examining the "bad spirits," as Oprah put it, that can poison the relationship with one's significant other a little bit at a time. The female half of one of the guest couples was a white, middle-class woman in her late twenties or early thirties who kept a meticulously detailed journal of what she and her husband each contributed to the upkeep of their marriage, ranging from how regularly she gave him sex, to who washed the dishes, took out the garbage, paid bills, provided treats and presents. It was an amazing display of minute scorekeeping driven not so much by the need for fairness and equity, or even a need to be able to document rightness in contentious arguments, but by pain so deep and frozen, so huge and debilitating that it pulsed through the television screen.

At one point during his questioning, Phil McGraw asked her why she might want to stop her journal keeping ways and I blurted out, with feeling, "It's no fun!" A split second behind me, as I clapped my hand to my mouth, surprised by my spontaneous outburst, the woman herself answered, "It's no fun." Something in me had actively identified with her compulsion and misery. Somehow, I had become involved with her process of uncovering obscured emotional realities and needs. As she was led into greater understanding, I was further touched by how the desire for mutual love and partnership that primally motivated her was the same desire—differently scripted and played—that impels so much of all our lives. Neither Oprah nor Phil pointed out that this woman's beginning breakthrough contained the potential for opening her mind and heart and fostering closer contact with her spirit-inspired capacity for truer, more generous and widespread loving of herself and others. But this potential was there, and it is what gives these mini-stories and events their real significance. Words with accompanying pictures flashed across the screen between segments: "Remembering Your Spirit . . . the Light in You . . . the Diva in You . . . the Child in You."

Finally, it should be noted that Oprah is an African American woman who predominantly features white people on her show, but who also does many things that reveal her racial commitment— things beyond bringing well-known figures such as Toni Morrison, Nelson Mandela, and Della Reese to the program. On her official Web site, for example, she lists topics in progress for upcoming programs, inviting those who are interested to tell their relevant stories and appear on the show. In late November 2000, there were twenty-one special topics in addition to the regular features. Situated among subjects titled "If You Had ONE Wish...," "Overcoming Your Fear," "Turning Down a Job," and others that related to home and holidays, there were three topics directly focused on race: "Lessons about Race," "Martin Luther King Jr.," and "Has Racism Changed You?"

"Lessons about Race" will deal with "people who have learned a lesson about racism and are sharing what they learned in unique and special ways." "Has Racism Changed You?" is seeking "people who have had to confront racism in their lives and became better people because of it." In both cases, the emphasis is relentlessly personal—what has been done "on a *personal* level to change yourself or your own behavior," "people who have overcome very *personal* struggles with racism" (italics mine).

This emphasis on the personal is fine and valid in that transformation begins with each individual's decision to change, and no one can accomplish her best work in the world until her own house is in order. However, exclusive reliance on a personal approach does not usually lead to consideration and/or discussion of the larger systemic and institutional factors that engender and perpetuate racism (and other societal ills like homelessness and poverty)—factors such as corporate greed and exploitation that support a mushrooming prison industry built on warehousing people of color; or a two-party political system which ensures that mostly white men with access to large sums of money will continue to rule the country through laws that reflect their limited minority interests and perspectives.

Oprah's Angel Network has awarded thousands and thousands of dollars to visionary individuals who are struggling to reverse the effects of systemic and institutional oppression through projects that feed, house, educate, and uplift those in need. Viewers are likewise encouraged to "use their life in service," to take their lives and use them "to the benefit of others," to "look inside themselves, see what they have to offer and use that to give back to the world." But the interlocking mega-systems of oppression remain hidden in the background while the personal heroism and vision are highlighted. Again, we should all be doing everything good that we can in our little corners of the world, but we must also have some greater, more impersonal and operative understanding of why the world is as it is.

This absence of greater context is similar to the fact that no one spelled out for the wife who clung to her scorekeeping journal the relationship between her own nascent awakening and her larger spiritual evolution. In both cases, we are presented with a lot of what is true and what we need to see, but we ourselves have to furnish background and implications and take what we are given a step further. Since all viewers cannot or do not choose to do this, I wish that Oprah would. Then we could all begin to anticipate the giant changes that even small but earth-shaking first steps might lead to—for instance, the journaling woman herself, minus her notebook and her pain, receiving one of Oprah's Angel awards for a splendid service project she has begun in her community; or the collective spiritual enlightenment fostered by *The Oprah Winfrey Show* as contributing to a revolution in consciousness akin to that which abolished segregation in the U.S. South or apartheid in South Africa.

Oprah's inclusion of topics about racism and her philanthropic social consciousness serve as a reminder that, for many African American women, their spirituality encompasses their politics as well as their creativity. In the mission statement for her show, Oprah explains: "I am guided by the vision of what I believe this show can be. Originally our goal was to uplift, enlighten, encourage, and entertain through the medium of television. Now, our mission statement for *The Oprah Winfrey Show* is to use television to transform peoples' lives." Without a doubt, Oprah looms large on the screen of contemporary culture as a racially committed, progressive, and spiritual African American woman. In her inimitable and important way, she models the central role black women play in furthering spirituality as we step into the twenty-first century.

Knocking at the Yellow House: Spiritual Daughters in Film

On the first day that she moved to her new hometown of Atlanta, Georgia, Toni Cade Bambara took a walk, found herself on Laughton Street, and saw a yellow house. "A yellow house?" she said to herself, "Well, for goodness sakes, let me knock on *that* door." And, "of course," the kind of person who would live in a yellow house was glad to see her. As Toni described that person during our interview, she turned out to be "a moon lady," "very, very Christian-based," who gave workshops to instruct people in effective prayer.

A bit later, as we were talking, Toni made a remark that assumed everyone moved through their lives in a spontaneously natural and spiritually guided fashion, compelling me to remind her that not everybody possesses the kind of intuitive spirituality that knocks at the door of a yellow house. She instantly responded: "I know everybody doesn't, but I also know millions who do." So saying, she launched into a discussion of the spiritual giftedness that is manifested in Julie Dash's 1991 film, *Daughters of the Dust,* and in other works by "sister filmmakers." Toni was making the point that African American women available to the call of spirit increasingly express their spirituality in movies and film. Thus, filmmaking by black women becomes another, important site of the self-reflexive, expanded spiritual consciousness that has arisen during the 1980s and 1990s and is continually taking shape in many forms.

Toni most certainly would have taken note of this lively cinematic activity. In addition to her career as a writer, she worked as a videographer and conducted script workshops for service organizations training to use video as a tool for social change. After she left Atlanta, for instance, she helped to plan, scripted, and narrated *The Bombing of Osage,* a film that documented the 1985 bombing of the radical Africanist group MOVE's settlement, a violent show of force carried out by the mayor and police in her new hometown of Philadelphia. Furthermore, as an avid consumer of movies since her childhood, she keenly monitored developments in this area. Thus, as we talked, she easily proffered film criticism, spiritual insight, and social analysis, all at the same time. From her authoritative seat, she particularly praised the innovative work of contemporary African American women filmmakers.

As an example of spirituality in black women's films, Toni cited Zeinabu irene Davis's production in which audiences encounter altars on the screen; the invocation of Yoruban deities; and sex presented as metaphor for the holiness of the body, spirit, power, and union. When an enthusiastic viewer who had just seen one of Davis's films mentioned that this was the first time she had ever witnessed a movie where there were altars, especially handled so casually and naturally, Toni was able to "rattle off" to her thirty such films. According to Toni, the way spiritual material is dealt with in independent cinema differs markedly from the way spiritual material is dealt with in the commercial sector. In commercial films, authentic black spirituality (what Toni termed the "culturally specific relationship we have to that power") is the "first thing" erased. Once erased, it is then put back into the film in false and surreptitious forms—"in disguise as enthusiasm (to use the ancient word)," or hidden underneath the music, or dumped into "Grandma, broken down Grandma with the broken down couch" as a type of "religious thing" or obligatory ancestral figure. Independent African American women filmmakers such as Zeinabu irene Davis counter this commercial mode.

Toni Cade Bambara's remarks about the world of film help call our attention to the fact that a number of contemporary black women are making movies that combine general cinematic excellence with beautifully portrayed spiritual themes and materials. That this is so became strikingly evident with the 1991 release of *Daughters of the Dust,* Julie Dash's extraordinary film about a Gullah family from the Carolina sea islands crossing over into mainstream life. Around 1980 (that potent and pivotal year), after her third short work, *Illusions,* Dash "committed herself to producing films about black women at various times in history" and began thinking about the project that eventually became *Daughters.* In every step of the production, she took pains to imbue her creation with, to use her words, "magic and mystery." To musically convey that magic and mystery, she chose John Barnes to compose the original score. He drew from his own spiritual beliefs, including a respect for astrology, to write the music, utilizing myriad instruments and musical expressions to depict various religions—from traditional West African worship rituals, to Santeria, Islamic, Catholic, and Baptist traditions. In her essay on making *Daughters,* Dash further explains, interspersing her comments with quotes from John Barnes:

> For instance, he [John] wrote the "Unborn Child's" theme in the key of B, the key of Libra, representing balance and justice. "This character was coming into the world to impart justice, a healing upon her father and her mother and her family." Similarly, he wrote "Nana's Theme" in the key of A, representing the Age of Aquarius, or the new age that was imminent for Nana's family.
>
> The closing theme, called the "Elegba Theme," was written in the key of Taurus, D sharp (or E flat). John told me, "It is the key of the earth, the key ruled by love." The lyrics, "Ago Elegba . . . show the way, Elegba," he says, are about people who are moving forward after having been given love and dignity, and who are now facing the crossroads.

The leadership and care that Dash exhibited in making sure the music for *Daughters of the Dust* was as perfect as possible is indicative of her work in all other aspects of the film. The strength of her spiritual motivation and vision resulted in a creation that Toni Cade Bambara enthusiastically supported and that Masani Alexis DeVeaux praised, not just for its "ability to be in touch with the folk ways, the roots," but for its "ability to construct ourselves in such a way that we are psychically powerful." Through her achievement, Dash further opened the way for other "sister filmmakers."

Eve's Bayou versus Soul Food: Making Waves in a Tide of Gender

Seven years after *Daughters of the Dust,* Kasi Lemmons's film, *Eve's Bayou,* appeared in progressive theaters across the country. The work of a young black woman actress-turned-screenwriter and director, this remarkable movie highlights many issues that pertain to African American women's role as conductors of spiritual power in the twenty-first century. It is an original and historically respectful exploration of diverse African American spiritual traditions, which tackles, in a deft and sophisticated manner, such femininely resonant topics as sexual abuse and the possibilities of personal freedom for women. It expands our consideration of the new spirituality of black women beyond the realm of lived experience and books into the equally important arena of visual media, in this case film. And, finally, because of the reception it received in the official African American community as represented by the NAACP, it reveals the difficulty that visionary black women often face in having their insights and talents appreciated.

In order to discuss these issues more graphically, I will contrast *Eve's Bayou* with another film that also appeared in 1998— *Soul Food.* This movie, which enjoyed a good deal of popularity at mainstream houses, was written and directed by George Tillman Jr. and inspired by the hit recording, "A Song for Mama," by Kenneth "Babyface" Edmonds, who was also the film's executive producer. In the final analysis, *Soul Food* is an example of what Toni Cade Bambara noticed regarding the disguise of black spirituality as a bogus grandmotherly or otherwise ancestral figure. However, to really see the difference in how spiritual matters are conceptualized and treated in these two films—one male-made and commercial, the other independent and female—requires taking a rather detailed look at the both of them.

Soul Food tells the story of the Joseph clan—the widowed matriarch Mama Jo, or Big Mama, and her three daughters, Maxine, Terry, and Bird. Max, who wears the mantle of the "strongest one," derives her identity from being wife of Kenny and mother of their children, the oldest of whom is Ahmad, who narrates the film. Terry, a money-conscious, high-powered lawyer, is married to Miles, also a lawyer, who is dissatisfied with his fast-track career and is letting it slide to devote himself to playing keyboards and leading a pop-soul band. Bird is a beautician with her own shop, trying to maintain financial security for herself and her ex-felon husband Lem, who gets fired from his job because of his prison conviction.

For forty years, the family has observed Sunday dinner at Big Mama's house, where the women have cooked together in the kitchen and everyone has eaten, fought, and been corrected by Mama around the table. Big Mama's culinary skill is legend. She wins hearts with her chicken and dumplings, neck bones, greens, black-eyed peas, deep-fried catfish, ham, macaroni and cheese, fried chicken, string beans, lima beans, corn on the cob, cornbread, and special egg pie. In the film, mouthwatering shots of all these dishes abound. Family crisis is precipitated when Mama, a diabetic not faithfully taking her medicine, has to have a leg amputated and, during the surgery, suffers a major stroke.

As she lies in a coma for five weeks, the family falls apart, riven by sexual infidelities, disputes about money, and all the hurts and differences that had simmered for years beneath the Mama-soothed surface. These tensions are further exacerbated when she dies.

In order to bring everyone back together, young Ahmad, whose voice leads us through this morass, concocts a hoax to gather them all at Big Mama's house for a Sunday meal. When his dish towel on the stove catches the house afire, and the hidden money that has lured each of them there becomes a found reality, they weather this flaming denouement and finally iron out the most corrosive acid from their differences. In the end, they maintain Mama's house and her tradition of family soul-food dinners.

Visually, plot-wise, and thematically, *Eve's Bayou* contrasts markedly with the straightforward melodrama of *Soul Food*. Set in south Louisiana, Eve's story is also retrospectively placed before us. A now grown-up Eve presents the summer during the 1960s when, as she states it, at the age of ten she killed her father. Louis Batiste, her father, is the black doctor of the town, suave, good-looking, and given to philandering with his female patients. Eve's elegant mother, Roz, is hard pressed to endure her doctor-husband's absences, but nevertheless maintains their materially comfortable way of life. Eve has a fourteen-year-old sister, Cicely, and a nine-year-old brother, Po. The extended family consists of her father's mother, who lives with them, and his attractive, thrice-widowed sister Mozelle, who does psychic "counseling" from her own home.

One night at the height of tension between Eve's parents, Louis comes home tipsy as usual and they have an awful fight.

Wanting to ease her father, whom she adores, Cicely steals downstairs and sits on his lap. We are never clear about exactly what happens next, as her memory and his memory do not match. Cicely believes that her father began kissing her as he would a woman, but he later swears in a letter to Mozelle that Cicely made these advances toward him and that he slapped her away. Regardless, Cicely goes into a depression and leaves home for a while, after telling her version of that night to Eve. Eve decides to kill her father for hurting Cicely and enlists the aid of the local voodoo practitioner, Elzora. When Eve changes her mind, she belatedly rushes back to Elzora (who has already symbolically buried Louis's coffin), then runs to the local juke joint and finds her father carrying on with Mattie Moreau, the lush, fun-loving wife of a young professor who is frequently away at school.

Because of insinuations that Eve has dropped on him at the market, Mattie's husband Lenny, drunk on alcohol and toting a pistol, also comes to the bar the very same night. He drags his wife away and warns Louis not to speak another word to her. Making light of the situation in his suave, superior style, Louis bids both Lenny and Mattie goodnight as they part outside, but Lenny suddenly snaps, pulls out his gun, and shoots Louis as Eve watches, horrified. After the funeral, Eve finds Louis's letter defending himself. He says he may be a small-town doctor, a pusher of pills who needs the adulation of women to be a certain kind of hero; and he may be guilty of letting his daughter dote on him far too much; but he would never, could never ever sexually molest his precious girl. Confronting Cicely, Eve uses her growing psychic ability—like that of her Aunt Mozelle—to read her sister. Seeking the truth, she finds out instead that Cicely's memory is a blurry, ambiguous haze. There is no simple black-and-white truth, no easily arrived at peace or closure. Thus the movie ends, with lingering shots of the tree-banked Mississippi River suggesting the continuous flow of life.

At the outset, beginning with its title, *Soul Food* sets us up to expect that the movie will deal with both a mundane and a spiritual exploration of "food" and "nourishment." The film delivers on the mundane in a grossly disappointing fashion, and it totally fails on the spiritual level. What spiritual hunger is, and what satisfyingly feeds it, is never truly expressed. There is a quick, initial statement about African American people learning how to make things like chitterlings taste good, and a definition of soul food as "cooking from the heart." Then, at the end, there is another brief, editorializing remark about cooking becoming the way, since slavery, that we have "expressed our love for one another." Thus, there is this historical contextualizing and this superficial equating of food and love. However, the possibilities that exist for doing something meaningful with these ideas are lost in the movie.

The basic Christian doctrine providing the religious overlay of *Soul Food* teaches that Christ is the real food of life and enacts this spiritual fact through the ritual of holy communion, where His body and blood are symbolically consumed. No character in the movie rises to this level of understanding. Nor is an earthly level of common sense on display. Its absence is blatant in the plot of the movie itself. Mama is a diabetic having her leg amputated, and then she dies of a stroke. All of these conditions are related to diet, particularly to the ingestion of pork, salt, sugar, and fat. Yet, even with Mama as a grisly example, the film still hypes "soul food," toxically high in illness-producing ingredients. After her death, Big Mama is memorialized, so to speak, with a dinner of the very food that killed her—and no one in the movie seems to have a clue.

I rave at this so-called "black love and spirituality" film for encouraging this behavior. Ultimately, any spiritual dimensions in *Soul Food* are just veneer and stereotype. There is, predictably, the greasin' buffoon of a preacher. He says comic grace at the dinner table and wins all the eating contests. A kind of spirituality is provided by the telepathic connection that apparently exists between Ahmad and Big Mama. Alone in the hospital room with Big Mama after she has lapsed into the coma, Ahmad speaks aloud to her, conversationally, and responsively, indicating that he is likewise hearing what she has to say. However, this connection is not contextualized in the movie by other instances of closeness between the two or by any other displays of psychic perceptiveness on Ahmad's part. Though he comes in as narrator at crucial junctures, he is really only a sweet observant kid, watching the obvious displays of immaturity and irresponsibility among the adult members of his family. It takes no supernatural prescience to know that when Bird gets her ex-boyfriend Simmie, who still wants her, to find a job for her husband Lem that some negative consequence will result.

In its handling of spiritual themes and moral issues, *Eve's Bayou* is light-years ahead of *Soul Food*. The audience learns immediately that Eve is a "woman of power" looking back at that unforgettable summer when she was ten and "killed her father." Whether she is actually guilty of his death is as complex a question as whether Louis made sexual advances toward Cicely. True, at one point, Eve wished her father dead so passionately that she consulted the voodoo worker. But was Elzora's spell effective, or did Louis effect his own demise at the hands of Mattie's cuckolded husband? Or, possibly, did some larger hand shuffle the deck? Yet, even at ten, Eve, like her slave ancestress, has the "gift of sight," of two-headed vision. This is clearly displayed in the scene where Eve's Aunt Mozelle shies away from the power and revelations emanating from her young niece's hands, and also in the scene at the end where Eve holds out her hands, compelling Cicely's, and psychically reads her sister. Earlier in the movie, Eve's dreams and visions were already shown to have come true.

There are other, equally rich, spiritual dimensions to the film. Mozelle is a gifted psychic counselor. She reads energy and channels images from the astral and perhaps higher planes. Before a reading, she sincerely prays—acknowledging that "we are all servants of divine will," herself included—as she seeks to ascertain that will and then gently and humanely passes it on to her troubled clients. Elzora, as voodoo lady, represents a black cultural tradition, one way that diasporic African people have used to try to put themselves in relation with spirit and exercise superhuman power. Though her character is informed by knowledge and treated with dignity, her way is, I think, shown to be a lesser path since it traffics in secrecy, fear, revenge, and other base human emotions. However, the power inherent in Elzora's trained use of energy is still validated, and this validation is metaphysically accurate, since energy is simply energy, power simply power, ultimately dependent for its qualities on how it is used.

Furthermore, the film presents deep, philosophical speculation about the meaning of existence. Musing aloud about life, Mozelle says there must be a divine point, somewhere just over her head. Or no point, and that's the point. Since most people's lives are a great disappointment to them and filled with pain, she says, if there is no explanation for it at the end, how sad.

Such speculation contrasts sharply with the one potentially meaningful message that emerges from *Soul Food*, when Ahmad recalls that his grandmother always admonished, "love yourself." Yet, nowhere are we given any suggestion that he or anyone else has a glimmer of what that means—not even at Aretha Franklin's level of knowing in her iconic song: the first way to spell love is R-E-S-P-E-C-T, for the self and for others.

In *Eve's Bayou*, the philosophical and metaphysical depth even extends into the cinematography. At one point, Mozelle recounts an intensely dramatic story about her first husband to Eve. At the place in the story where her illicit lover confronts her husband in their home, Mozelle, through a hallway mirror, enters the frame and simultaneously narrates and acts out the parts. The result is a breathtaking statement about the interpenetration of past and present, about the all-when, all-where, all-one nature of the spiritual universe.

Finally, in the character of Mozelle the film shows the possibility of redemption. Mozelle describes herself as "cursed" because her three husbands have died violent and premature deaths. If she is—if somehow, for some unknown reason, life has dealt her a tragic hand—then that darkness is dispelled by the grace that eventually comes to her in the form of love. A man named Julian Grayraven shows up on her doorstep in a rainstorm, pursuing information about the wife who has left him. He ends up painting a portrait of Mozelle and staying with her. There he finds peace and they fall in love. He eventually wants to locate his deserting wife so that he can divorce her and marry Mozelle. When Mozelle protests, damning herself as both barren and a curse, he renames her "wounded" and pledges to plant his seeds of love in her heart. Mozelle has a deeply affirmative dream of flying following her brother Louis's funeral. The dream tells her to let her former self die without looking back—so she answers yes to Grayraven's proposal and bets on life, on the love that is God, that is good, that is truth, that is light—the love that is the antidote for all kinds of spells and curses. While there is copulation aplenty in *Soul Food,* nowhere is there anything nearly as romantic and salvific as Grayraven's tender love.

In all matters, including the spiritual, *Soul Food* plays to the lowest common denominator. *Eve's Bayou,* on the other hand, gives us much of worth to think about. It encourages us to seek meaning beyond our limited, personal selves, which is the essence and definition of spirituality. It encourages us to apply these larger perspectives to, and adopt a detached, philosophical viewpoint toward our "little" lives. For instance, it causes viewers to question: What is memory, What is truth? What *really happened* that night between Louis and Cicely lies somewhere in the crevices between their memories—fogged by alcohol, adolescence, and the complex love between father and daughter. There are no easy answers to complicated moral questions. In the final voice-over, Eve tells us as much. She says she has the gift of sight, but that the truth changes color, depending on the light, and tomorrow can be clearer than yesterday. Memory, a collection of images, threads itself into a tapestry and texture that tell the story of our past.

This story of our past, as well as the present and future, is what she, as a psychic, reads. She scours the nonphysical planes, looking for helpful truths, no doubt striving for a clarity and wisdom even greater than her aunt's or her slave ancestor's, seeking higher and purer, finer and more refined levels of knowing, pursuing the place where truth and spirit shine clear. Saying that her "tomorrow can be clearer than yesterday" seems to be a graphic way of speaking about such generational and evolutionary progress.

The writers and directors respectively of *Eve's Bayou*, Kasi Lemmons, and *Soul Food*, George Tillman Jr., were both straining toward ideas in the all-divine, the all-creative, ideas pertaining to the meaning of family and family relations and how love plays itself out in these contexts. Aquarian New Age consciousness is about group sense and the influx of love. Hence, since families represent our first and most crucial group relations, and since the love we are able to exhibit as adults hinges on what we are taught about love as children in families of whatever kind, then clearly Lemmons and Tillman were attempting to deal with very important matters. What they create out of what they apprehend, however, shows, as did the examples in chapter 4, that how something is rendered into form, how it is given manifested shape, depends upon the innate gifts and acquired skill of the receiver.

Knocking at the door of the yellow house was Toni Cade Bambara's way of talking about spiritual attunement. Yellow is the color of the third chakra, which is the stomach and solar plexus center. It has to do, of course, with food and other appetites, but it is also thought to be the seat of the will in animals and emotionally polarized human beings. Therefore, when we encounter this "yellow" region, we meet issues of self-governance and appropriate functioning of personality willpower. (Recall, for example, how the epithet, "yellow-bellied" is employed in traditional Hollywood westerns.) The two movies discussed above put before us the question: At that chakra level, do we have the necessary will, the requisite self-control? If what is required is achieved, we would stop messing over and killing each other, and we could start being servants of divine will rather than our own petty gods and goddesses. Then, and only then, can we knock at the doors of expanded and potential consciousness. This would help lift us to the seventh and highest chakra, where spiritual guidance holds sway. Interestingly, in Julie Dash's *Daughters of the Dust* one of the major characters, Yellow Mary, was forced into prostitution at an early age, and now exhibits decency and kindness based upon her own understanding of a higher type of moral law.

I attribute Lemmons's crafting of the film *Eve's Bayou*, which is spiritual in the largest sense of the word and inspires us to depth and growth, to her attunement with the New Age energies motivating African American women to an unprecedented degree. Tillman works on a different level in *Soul Food*, one that is more backward-looking than future-oriented, which shows the truth in statements that women are carrying the spiritual power at this present, transitional time. Having noted this personally when I watched these films, I would probably not have done anything further with it, except that, on a March 1998 visit to my mother in Louisiana, I happened to catch the televised NAACP Image Awards. Unfortunately—or fortunately—viewing the ceremony spun me back into the disbelieving and thoughtful state I had experienced when I first saw *Soul Food*.

This movie and those associated with it won award after award. The writer-director George Tillman Jr., was cited. The young actor, Brandon Howard, who played Ahmad, strode confidently across the stage for his recognition. Kenneth "Babyface"

Edmonds, whose hit "A Song for Mama" inspired the movie and who was its executive producer, received awards. Meanwhile, Kasi Lemmons, the writer-director of *Eve's Bayou;* Jurnee Smollett, the young actress who was spectacular in the role of Eve; Eryka Badu, who provided vocals; and other personnel instrumental in producing the film were repeatedly passed over as they sat in the audience or even, adding insult to injury, as they went onstage themselves to announce or hand out awards. I could not believe what I was seeing. Why was the brilliance of *Eve's Bayou* not being recognized?

Eventually, I had to answer, because it was just that—too brilliant. It required these entrenched African American powers-that-be to place their seal of approval on a product that called for something other than mindless digestion of standard fare and stereotypes. They were much more comfortable singing along with Babyface's lyrics: "Mama, you're the queen of my heart / Mama, loving you is like food to my soul"—which also brought in the emotional, economic, and seemingly hip, grassroots validation of black pop-soul music.

There is also the fact that the exploration of family in *Eve's Bayou* hinges not solely on simplistic parental love and marital infidelity, but also on the topic of child sexual abuse. Even though the film is very sympathetic to Louis Batiste, the treatment of this subject is handled very ambiguously (if anything, the weight of truth is leveraged on Louis's side), it was probably still too close to home, too near to the bone for many black men. Further, for both women and men, it may have been a shade too touchy or potentially controversial—especially for those who would see even so tasteful an invocation of this prevalent problem as black-feminist male-bashing. And, finally, I do not believe it is possible to overestimate the force of sexist norms and masculinist control. Those responsible for *Soul Food* were mostly men; those for *Eve's Bayou* mostly women. And, except for the prodigiously talented Samuel L. Jackson in the role of Dr. Louis Batiste, females dominated the latter film.

As New Age emissaries, Kasi Lemmons and other African American women like her are calling us to apply critical consciousness to ourselves and our spiritual traditions, to continue to celebrate what is enduring and useful about them, and to either infuse old forms with new life or cast them out. The thinking that is represented by the laden table, long-suffering grandmother, and a parodied, superficial Christianity of *Soul Food* needs serious revitalization. By contrast and example, this is the message of change that *Eve's Bayou* and similar works are bringing to us, a message that is thoroughly in step with the rapidly turning times. It makes me happy to be able to say, in closing, that Lemmons's cinematic gem became the most financially successful independent film released in 1997 and that critic Roger Ebert—who, ironically, sat in the audience at the NAACP Image Awards ceremony applauding *Soul Food*—chose *Eve's Bayou* as the year's best film.

And Women Continue to Offer Transformation

In *Soul Talk,* I am, of course, specifically concerned with the role African American women are playing in the rise of New Age spiritual consciousness at this present time when humanity in general is attempting to transition from the waning Piscean to the waxing Aquarian age. However, in this chapter built on the thesis that women as a whole have a special and heightened role in this massive transformation, it seems to me appropriate to examine the very visible example of this female role as presented by outgoing First Lady—now Senator—Hillary Rodham Clinton. In doing so, I am making no claims about the type or degree of her personal spirituality. Nevertheless, I have been struck by what I could see of her tendencies toward being open to the kind of New Age understandings and practices that are increasingly commonplace in society at large but not acknowledged in official national policy or pronouncements. In the White House—that domestic fishbowl that functions as a strange macrocosmic microcosm—she exhibited in two notable instances the female potential for spiritual transformation, while the weighty institutional apparatus surrounding her conspired to subvert her movement in enlightened directions.

In 1996, before his pre-election popularity surge, President Clinton was made more anxious because of the media attention focused on Mrs. Clinton's relationship with Jean Houston, philosopher, "sacred psychologist," human potentialist, and co-director of the Foundation for Mind Research, which studies psychic and altered states. In meetings with Houston, Hillary Rodham Clinton had engaged in imaginary conversations with Eleanor Roosevelt and Mahatma Gandhi as a strategy to amplify her own personal power and mission during a time in 1995 when she felt beleaguered and depleted.

Mrs. Clinton's association with Houston was not unusual. The Clintons had already become the first First Family to, as *Newsweek* magazine phrased it, "welcome alternate psychologies and New Agey management techniques," represented by such guru-like personages as Michael Lerner, Marianne Williamson, Anthony Robbins, and Stephen Covey. However, because this particular incident was highly publicized in Bob Woodward's book *The Choice* and smacked a little of channeling, it unnerved and embarrassed the White House enough for them to downplay it and cut connections with Houston.

However, it is not clear to me who the White House thinks is being turned off by such things. Even *Newsweek* points out that the kind of "exercises in personal transformation the Clintons have been sampling" is mainstream:

> Houston herself has run seminars for the Department of Commerce and other federal agencies. At Stanford Business School, Prof. Michael Ray has prepared future captains of industry with Tarot cards and chants to release their deepest selves. Indeed, the fastest buck in the motivational marketplace no longer goes to successful football coaches but to organizational gurus who have discovered happiness and productivity. . . . If CEOs can enhance their potential, isn't it natural that the nation's chief executive and his spouse would try to augment theirs?

In addition, the magazine gives mini-profiles of a forty-nine-year-old hospital administration consultant who uses the Ouija board and her ability to see auras to find key personnel; a couple in Minneapolis who lead a neo-Masonic group in studying the consciousness-enhancing teaching of Armenian mystic G. I. Gurdjieff (whom students of African American literature will recognize as the spiritual teacher of Jean Toomer, author of *Cane*); and Horst Rechelbacker, CEO of the Aveda beauty salon chain, who considers his company his "spiritual practice" and is devoted to shamanic journeying.

A full 40 percent of people polled for the *Newsweek* article "admitted to believing in the supernatural." Feature coverage for what the editors termed "out there"— meaning *The X-Files* television series, the film *Independence Day,* and paranormal phenomena in general—revealed that 48 percent of Americans believe UFOs are real and 29 percent think that we have already made alien contact. It was during these same 1996 midsummer months that newly discovered solar systems dramatically increased the possibility of other life systems in the universe. And, for whatever it may suggest to potentially progressive presidents such as Mr. Clinton, another 48 percent believe there is a government plot to cover up the extraplanetary contact.

The White House's reluctance to be too closely associated with these nontraditional technologies that push consciousness into spiritual realms beyond the everyday ordinary human, looks to me like yet another instance of misplaced timidity where an unwavering adherence to the new ground that grows from bright, right impulses would better serve. During high-tide times, President Clinton and Hillary seemed to be open and expansive. In times of perceived threat and insecurity, they retreated toward what is conservative. As the first family, they could entertain Jean Houston and the other New Age prophets, but, in September 1998, when President Clinton had to confess to an escapade with intern Monica Lewinsky and bear the judgmental fallout, he sought what his press people referred to as "pastoral counseling," something infinitely more conventional and supposedly reassuring to the American public.

This same pattern of an enlightened move by the first lady,

followed by retrograde media coverage, leading to recanting and retrenchment, was again displayed when, in her mid-1999 interview with *Talk* magazine, Mrs. Clinton made a connection between her husband's string of marital infidelities and his troubled childhood. She simply stated the obvious: The emotional abuse that scarred young Bill in his dysfunctional family—an alcoholic stepfather who sometimes threatened his mother; an erratic maternal grandmother who partially raised him during his mother's absence and tried to get legal custody of him (at age four) because she was outraged by her daughter's second marriage; young Bill Clinton's vulnerable and tenuous position in the midst of all this—contributed to his confused dealings with women and his general personality weaknesses. It is not unusual for people today to draw such parallels routinely—and not just in a psychiatrist's office.

Even before the magazine hit the newsstands, reporters were clamoring for comment from the White House, and White House spokespeople were gradually shifting and reframing what Hillary had said. Her remarks negatively impacted the masculinized presidential image and, in addition, political pundits were taking them at everything but their face value and discrediting her. This was unfortunate; the "channeling" incident, the Lewinsky scandal, and the interview flap could all have been opportunities for the Clintons as first family to educate the press and public and to model new, spiritualized approaches to life and living.

Evolutionary energies may be pushing humankind toward clarity and refinement regarding sex and sexuality. Opening to this principled, New Age perspective could have suggested to President Clinton innovative ways to proceed, ways that would have earned him the place in history as a great president that his soul desires. This could have included not confessional disclosure but total honesty and explanation; guidance from a cadre of psychic, astrological, shamanic, and similar advisors who know how to read something other than the latest poll; acknowledgment of dysfunctional emotional patterns acquired in childhood and therapeutic work to heal them; no tit-for-tat blaming but thoughtful discussion of how his situation represented a shared and common problem crying to be addressed by revolutionarily different notions about the meaning of marriage and sexual union; not penitential religious solace, but a bold sense of working cooperation with transformative spiritual energies.

Imagine how much good would have been served if, instead of trying to blunt Mrs. Clinton's interview remarks about the link between her husband's tumultuous childhood and his adult behavior, the White House had referenced work by leading mainstream and transpersonal psychologists to further contextualize and support what she said. Unfortunately, we have not yet progressed to a place where this can happen at the level of our nation's leader. Overall, the relentless, two-term bombardment of President Clinton by conservative elements reveals just how difficult it is for creative innovation to prevail. In the midst of his national initiative on race, what received attention *ad nauseum,* beyond what the public wanted, was the Lewinsky matter—and I cannot believe that this is totally coincidental. To triumph in the face of old modes and mores requires a kind of courage that is difficult for a person with unresolved, unhealed issues to summon—no matter how intelligent, good-hearted, or charismatic he might be.

Still, more support, even yearning, for visionary thought and action abounds than old institutionalized paradigms presently accommodate. Like Iyanla, like Oprah, like Kasi Lemmons, African American women are acutely aware of themselves as spiritual beings within this critical, transitional context. Furthermore, the ways that black women manifest this beingness helps point the way toward a spirituality that is capable of cooperating with the many means through which spirit is attempting to dance within each of us on the planet, for us all.

ᘛ 7 ᘚ

CLOSING THE CIRCLE:
UNITING CREATIVE, SPIRITUAL, AND POLITICAL POWER

Having worked on political fronts to honor concrete identities and improve material realities, having developed a spiritual consciousness with its attendant creative results, how then do African American women pull it all together? Once accessed, how are spirituality and creativity then brought to bear on politics, but at a higher turn of the spiral? How are our triple energies—the spiritual, creative, and political—bonded into a complete circle for possible transformative change?

From the depths of desperate struggle, Michele Gibbs answers these questions by invoking the spiritual "seed inside" each and every one of us that "speaks to creativity and birth and continuance." Toni Cade Bambara formulates the concept of "availability," defined as willingness to put one's whole being at the disposal of divine, inexplicable forces and energies greater than the small, personality self. Once allegiance to these ideas is given, then, what does a life of commitment look like? How does it proceed? What are its issues, lessons, and rewards?

Responses to these questions emerge from what Sonia Sanchez and Geraldine McIntosh tell us about their work—Sonia as a poet and writer, and Geraldine as a human resources specialist at a multinational corporation. Lucille Clifton takes availability to an even higher level. In service to suprahuman, nonphysical beings, she channeled messages from The Ones Who Talk. Then, in her own role as poet, she represented the information and warnings that these Ones had given to her. They are ancient spiritual lessons of collective love and responsibility that, if creatively applied to our current, out-of-balance, and negatively political society, would totally alter global consciousness and redeem the world.

From Politicized Spirituality to Spiritualized Politics

Politics and spirituality are usually regarded as diametrically opposed disciplines. And even when they are not, the question becomes, what is their relationship to each other and how are the two to be melded? This question looms large for many African American women. Those of us who are conscious in both areas have no desire for any kind of spiritual practice that does not actively engage the alleviation of racial ills and injustice. Nor do we seek personal spiritual happiness and enlightenment that leaves the majority of our brothers and sisters in the dark. Just as spirituality has to encompass politics, we are beginning to envision a new kind of politics fundamentally grounded in spirituality and not simply strengthened by it. Michele Gibbs's movement from conceiving of social change based on Marxist analysis and traditional community organizing to possessing a more spiritually informed vision of what is necessary to achieve revolution illustrates the difference.

Michele began her life cradled in radical politics. Her father was a black man, born in Texas, who embraced Marxism and fought in Spain for the overthrow of Franco during World War II. Her mother, also Marxist, was a white, Jewish woman. Growing up as a "red-diaper baby," a child of interracial parents in Chicago during the 1950s, gave Michele an induction into the politics of race and class difficult to surpass. Taught to think for herself and find her own way, Michele, nevertheless, took on the worldview of her parents and committed herself to revolution. In addition to earning her Ph.D. in American Studies from Brown University, she fought for civil rights, women's liberation, and peace. In the early 1980s, she left the United States to help birth Maurice Bishop's vision of a free Grenada. All of this activity shows the depths of her allegiance to a material-based politics.

However, Michele gradually realized the limitations of this solely materialist approach. As early as 1979, when she left her adopted hometown of Detroit for Grenada, she knew that, in her words, "there was nothing [that had been tried] that could turn around the reality of Detroit for the majority of its people." And this has continued to be her perception. The failure of Bishop's New Jewel movement and his assassination, which included the U.S. invasion of Grenada in 1983, threw Michele into crisis and caused her to reevaluate the specifics of how she was living her life. A period of disengagement, followed by her moving out of the United States and reinstituting her talent as a creative artist, was the result. Now, in the face of ever-worsening conditions everywhere for all but the richest people, she clearly sees that there is what she considers to be only one, truly transformative way out for everyone still trapped in deprivation and despair. That is to reframe the questions, and look within for spiritual answers.

As she expressed it, "What do we do now? What do we do? How can we get a handle on not only our community but ourselves?" Having asked this basic question, she volunteered her response:

> I could only answer from my own experience, that is, I had to face the question of what am I here for, what is my work in this world, do I have a gift that is essentially me? Not what does anybody else expect of me. Not what does this other community need. No, the wrong questions. What is that essential seed inside me that speaks to creativity and birth and continuance? And once you identify that, you will see what to do. And my own belief is that everybody has that. But their belief in human nature is not always that strong—which is part of the problem.

In her desperate attempt to find a way to both live and struggle, Michele had to ask herself this basic question. She knew that, once this all-important dilemma was solved, right action benefiting both self and society would result. She couched the question in a metaphoric and spiritual fashion, using terms like "essential seed," "birth," and "creativity." With this response to her dilemma about a meaningful way to live, Michele arrived at the same place as Velma Henry, the protagonist in Toni Cade Bambara's 1980 novel, *The Salt Eaters*—that is, a place where spiritual reality must be honored and then impressed upon material reality so that necessary progress and healing can happen on personal and societal fronts.

Yet, this does not mean giving up on what Michele and I kept simplistically referring to as ordinary "black and white" life. She still returns each year to Detroit from her current home-in-exile, Oaxaca, Mexico. Now, however, both her perspective and the work that she undertakes in Detroit to make an impact are different. The only "sign of life," she observes, is in the musical community, comprised of people whose way of knowing and being has nothing to do with either the automobile industry or power politics, or anything that could be described as linear cause and effect. When she visits, she does performance poetry with them: "I really need to get to a different, below-the-conscious level with the people there, and to maintain my connections with those who are also at that level but who are stuck in the city."

Performing poetry with serious but free-spirited musicians is a very different activity than leafleting or demonstrating. Michele sees in it the possibility of making interventions in a more primary or, if you will, a more transcendent, sphere. In that place, she hopes to tap into a sense of group identity that is empowering. It is the same group identity that informs her art: "Most of the images in my artwork are an attempt to make our collective identity more visible to us. It assumes that we have a collective identity, for one thing, but that's one of my assumptions that I'm not giving up." As she explains it, she has always positioned herself in terms of "our," "us," and "we." However, the aggregate that these words have referred to has kept getting bigger and bigger. She started with the people on her block, the "us in Detroit" since 1970—"black folks, primarily poor folks, working people, certainly women who are trying to evolve new ways of being sane, people of whatever 'ethnic or racial group' they are born into, but whose operative identity crosses traditional boundaries."

That first "us" was matched by another segment of "us," composed of individuals "whose internal identity is self-generated and, when articulated, smashes the received categories." Included here are teachers who were redefining how learning was done, work that Michele and I were engaged in when we met during the mid-1970s. Asking a question like, "Why can't we study Nina Simone in universities?" is, as she phrases it, "an example of new categories of identity and value and validation." In addition, another such grouping has been the "autonomous women's movement," which was refusing to "capitulate to the accepted gender lines" and breaking new ground, ground that she would have termed ideological then but would call spiritual now, "because ideology is a very limited category in itself."

Finally, in her scheme, "us" has expanded to encompass all those who, "in spite of living in the so-called modern world, order their lives by means that transcend technology." They are people whose "life space is organic" and structured by "meaning which has nothing to do with the material world as such." Her immediate instance of this sensibility came from her current residence in Oaxaca where "people go around without shoes all the time. It's not because they can't afford shoes. It's because they want their feet to be on the ground—literally. There are other hardships that are imposed by material scarcity, which I'm not trying to romanticize. But there's an orientation that is organic which is, I really think, our only salvation."

When I asked her for an example from the United States of a trans-technological way of life manifesting itself, she responded by saying, "In our writing I see it." The writing she referred to is the body of work being produced by contemporary African American women, the groundbreaking, mindblowing explorations of both physical and metaphysical reality represented by such authors as Toni Morrison, Alice Walker, Toni Cade Bambara, Gayle Jones, Lucille Clifton, Sonia Sanchez, June Jordan, Gloria Naylor, Octavia Butler, Audre Lorde, Paule Marshall, Dolores Kendrick, Sherley Anne Williams, Ntozake Shange, as well as other younger or less well-known writers like SDiane Bogus, Tina McElroy Ansa, Shirley Jackson-Opoku, Jewelle Gomez, A. J. Verdelle, Devorah Major, Phyllis Alesia Perry, and many more. Michele is hopeful that this writing, in her words, will "open readers up to hidden recesses in themselves that they haven't tapped. That artistic expression, that body of work becomes a reality. It *is* reality. It *has* reality—not just for the writers, but for us. And it changes our reality."

Most definitely Michele has decided that the way to make change in the world is to "hit people below the conscious." For those whose visualization schematic operates in reverse, this is the same as saying "hit people above the rational." Without knowing whether or not her work accomplishes this aim, she hopes that it does because it is all that she can do. With this approach, at the very least, she is able to be more productive. She says, "the more my work develops, the more energy I have to do other kinds of things as well. Political work for me in the past has always been a very draining process. I find this just the opposite; it's an energizing process. So that tells me something. And if it can do that for me, maybe it can do that for other people." What she has found is that coming to her work from the inner orientation of the spiritual seed inside her and expressing that as best she can, has proven to be tremendously fruitful and liberating.

Still, what does one say to a staunchly committed worker like Sister Cynthia (not her real name) who continues to struggle as a member of traditional political organizations in Detroit? Cynthia is aware of the debilitation that comes from the manner in which males control traditional political structures even as she works among the growing homeless population. First of all, Michele points out, Sister Cynthia's efforts and the current concrete reality bear "no resemblance to the past. Forget point of production. What point of production? Ain't no production. What we're trying to produce is life, not surplus value." Confronted with a room of fifty homeless people, forty-five of whom are women and children, something entirely new has to transpire. Working with consciousness, the correct response becomes, *All right, now what kind of a home can we create together? What kind of an alternative model for the sustenance of life can we imagine?*

Michele and I explored this further in our discussion:

Michele: This is a totally different thing from like . . .

Akasha: Let's go picket City Hall and make them give us an old abandoned building. Well, it may get to that.

Michele: Well, it already has. Everything traditional has already been tried by very able people in Detroit, and nothing has worked.

Akasha: So it's really on the level of a vision, imagination, creativity.

Michele: Reimagining everything. What do I need in order to live, and by way of human community? What does it look like? What does it feel like? Where is the germ of it as we sit in this room?

Akasha: Okay, let's deal with what you imagine. I don't have any trouble myself with embracing the idea that change has to take place from that level now. But I guess I'm trying to figure out what if somebody still says, "Yeah, but the people have to have somewhere to lay their heads at night. And children still need milk."

Michele: First, people have to get real about what they need. I mean, is it baby formula? Is it Wonder Bread? What kind of milk? Certainly not from chemically fed cows. First, you have to get rid of all the junk that you're bombarded with in the society every day before more of it does you any good. More of it is not going to do any good. So, it requires a kind of fundamental altering of consciousness before we even know what won't help us. The other conclusion I've reached is that I really do believe in cycles of civilization, and this one will have to just destroy itself. And I'm trying to stay out of the way so it doesn't get me, too. Seriously. Because I think we just have to wait, I think we have to wait this little cycle out and lie low and build whatever supportive networks we can, and which will allow us to do that, extricate ourselves as much as possible from all the dependencies this society fosters, and then we can be free enough to start reimagining what we want to do. But you got to take yourself out of it before you can do anything else. And that's not a hippie solution.

Akasha: Yes, okay. There's a part of me that goes along with the cycle thing. Any fool with eyes can see that they're on a path of destruction that has to continue for some time longer. But there is this other part of me that likes to think and operate from the model that despite what they're doing, there is something very vital in the now, in the sort of alternative everything that we're about. Conceptualizing it like this highlights what is rising to oppose what is currently holding sway.

Michele: Oh, absolutely. And because the process, the alternative process is such a personal one, it's hard to see. But it's there.

Akasha: It's there, and that's part of what this conversation is about. It's about looking at how this is seen, just like you one, me one, all these others. There's a thing that's spreading. It's doing its work, you know, it's igniting, and it's a very palpable energy, a very powerful force that is operating in all kinds of ways to . . .

Michele: To free people.

With a fundamentally altered consciousness about what constitutes political work, we can return to Michele's root question: "What is that essential seed inside of me that speaks to creativity and birth and continuance?" That seed, she hopes, will sprout and grow into something programmatic and useful for all of us. To illustrate, Michele reminisced about having returned one year to Detroit only to find the entire community completely demoralized because the one man on whom they had pinned their future prospects had died young of a heart attack. She continued: "But when I came back the next year, some of those people had in fact moved to the point of asking themselves that question and beginning to find some answers in at least some tentative directions." The new avenues were "keeping them going," and they were not feeling guilty for "abandoning the cause." Michele opined that "the absence of any other alternatives" helped them to reach that point: "And I'm not romantic about this shit. I mean, when you can't do anything else, you figure out something else. It's just how we stay alive." Staying alive by nurturing the seed inside is a spiritual solution.

Now at the beginning of the twenty-first century, the need for this variety of spiritual consciousness has not been obviated. In the cycle of the last four to five decades, a great deal of forward motion has been accomplished through forceful action in the external world. Now, continuing progress in this same way is increasingly difficult to achieve. Longstanding dilemmas seem almost impossible to solve, and recalcitrant problems get worse and worse as retrograde elements gain temporary dominance. Affirmative action is being dismantled, the death penalty as selectively used against men of color is being revived, and marginalized women and children continue to free-fall without safety nets. It is these circumstances that forced Michele to foreground spirituality in the fight for social justice.

The Politics of Spiritual Availability

In *The Salt Eaters* Toni Cade Bambara powerfully addressed the necessity of deploying political and spiritual energies in tandem. Yet even Toni has been forced to look further into the dilemma of how to make major change. Her more recent work was guided by a question that, like Michele's, specifically lifted up the spiritual half of this politics-spirituality equation. She framed it for me during our interview in this way: "What happens to people with active pineal glands under the leadership of deadheads?" This provocative and timely question could be translated as, "What happens to spiritually awake and adept people in a world ruled by the unenlightened?" However, the mere fact that she couched her query in this way reveals her esoteric knowledge and provides an opportunity to discuss matters that interested her and informed her work, matters pertaining to the metaphysical significance of the pineal gland and to individuals who are capable of receiving high doses of energy from transpersonal, spiritual realms.

Atypical of many fiction writers, Toni majored in biochemistry and thought that at some point in her life she would become a medical doctor. Her scientific training provided the starting place for information that she takes to other, esoteric levels. The pineal gland she refers to is found uppermost in the endocrine system of ductless glands. Located at the very top of the head, at what we call the "soft spot" on a baby's skull, it corresponds to the seventh and topmost, or crown, chakra. Chakras are centers or openings in the etheric body through which flow the more subtle energies that determine the dense physical body. Western medicine knows less about the function of the pineal gland than it knows, for instance, about the sexual-reproductive chakra gonads, the insulin secreted by the pancreas in the solar plexus region, or the thyroid gland located in the throat. Old medical texts typically refer to the pineal gland as "vestigial" and note that whatever it does seems to fade during childhood.

Ancient wisdom teaches that the pineal gland is the "seat of the soul" because of its location at the point where the spiritual self intersects the physical body. A few years ago, the pineal gland made popular news because of discoveries about melatonin, the secretion it produces. Researchers found that melatonin, interacting with light, possesses sleep-inducing and age-retarding properties, a discovery that brought large numbers of people into drug and health food stores to buy it.

However, well before melatonin flashed on the scene as the newest supplement to become a fad, enlightened black scholars and scientists from a number of disciplines had stepped up their investigation of melanin, the pigmentation-producing material found in dark-skinned people. They found connections between melanin and the slowing down of the aging process and between melanin and emotional sensitivity and trancelike states. The researchers concluded that the secretion is definitely a transphysical component within the constitutional systems of black people and not simply a skin color factor.

Both the research about melanin and melatonin provide instances of modern science slowly piecing together hard data that rationally explains mystical knowledge and popular wisdom. The pineal gland and its controlling crown chakra constitute the channel through which a person reaches the higher self and spiritual realm. So, in effect, the question that Toni framed, stated yet a third way, is, "What happens to people whose spiritual consciousness has been (re)awakened to active usefulness in a society still predominantly run by those who have not been similarly energized?"

From a nondeterministic but racially informed perspective, Toni's query speaks to the wealth of spiritual potential inherent in black people, and it asks with concern about our psychic and spiritual well-being in an overwhelmingly white milieu. More universally, the question becomes: How does spirituality make a place for itself in a materially limited and materialistic world? The answer, or at least one important answer, emerged from my conversation with Toni. It is this: One way for pineal-active, spiritually conscious people to make a place for who they are and what they represent in the world is to be the opening, the channel, the site of connection to transpersonal, transcendent, metaphysical ideas and energies. As we talked further, serving in this way became encapsulated in the concept of "availability" or "being available."

In the very first exchange we had, once the tape recorder had been turned on, the concept of being "available" cropped up. Answering my question about why *The Salt Eaters* has such a compendious feel, Toni discussed the need she had at the time of its writing to draw in everything she knew:

> *Toni:* . . . to figure out as a community organizer working in a time when and a place where there are 800,000 regimens, codified systems of belief, therapeutic models, wisdoms, knowledges, available in the black community, some of which are tapped, some of which are ignored, some of which are suppressed. I seem to be . . . available to, yeah, a lot of those different things, those strains, those frames of references. If I pull them all together and look at them, I will know what my next step is, I will know how to create value.

> *Akasha:* I noticed that you stopped when you got to, and then found the words for, "I seem to be available to." Why did it take you so long to figure out how to say that?

Toni: Well, it has to do with how do you know what you know? The answer is, you don't. How do you gain knowledge? Many, many channels, some of which we have names for—intuition, channeling, visions, visitations—and other things we don't have names for. So I just say "available to."

A bit later on, we were wrangling over how she got "turned on" to spiritual knowledge. She insisted that there was never a time growing up in Harlem when she was not aware of "the dream book people," or "the people who can walk through trees," or "people who levitate." When I reminded her that tons of folks lived in those same neighborhoods without ever getting in touch with this information, she replied: "This gets back to the notion of available, and how do you know what you know? You don't. I don't. I'm available to it. I'm available to it." Increasingly engaged, she enlarged on the idea:

> I mean, this question of who gets made available. I don't know. When I look at, for example, someone like Ron Karenga, who has rather retrograde personal politics, but is clearly being visited by—what shall we call it? Some people call it a muse—by the spirit of African scholarship, we'll call it that; one might raise the question, "Why him? How does he get chosen by spirit to be the vehicle, the messenger for this very necessary thing we need to have?" I don't know. Or we look at Miles [Davis, the jazz trumpeter]. How does this guy, a self-professed woman-beater, why is he available to the gods of genius? I don't know. Maybe because he

practiced, maybe because he believed he was a genius. I don't know. And even as we read his autobiography, there is nothing in the autobiography—*clear* as he is about his own development. The question still remains, why you? How did you become available to the gods of genius?

Or you look at Billie Holiday [the legendary jazz singer]. My goodness, why didn't she just let the music go? It was killing her, wracking her, moving her into the drug thing. She couldn't handle it maybe. I'm about to say all kinds of dopey things. Why didn't she let it go? Why her? Why didn't she look that spirit in the eye and say, "Move this over somewhere. Don't run it through my body. Just put it in the air near me so I can reach for it and sing it, but don't run this shit through my body. Can't handle it."

Or Trane [jazz saxophonist John Coltrane]. Now the minute somebody comes along named Trane, for black people with all our traveling shoes and "Hey Mister Brakeman," and Amtrak Blues and Migration and Travel and Journey and all that stuff, they obviously are going to be given a mandate by the black community to develop their genius. If his name was Leroy Washington, he still could be a genius, but I don't know that we would have given him the arena. So here comes Trane, obviously on a mission, looking for a sound, looking for a walk or sound. He moves in that direction. He plays, I mean, he drives people around to nuts. He's after something that exists in his imagination. And he's chosen; that is to say, he reaches a point of sound spirit where he could make the journey. He's not afraid to make the journey. But in order to make that journey, his body gets wracked, and it gets to be a desperate search. And so next thing you know, he's on heroin.

As Toni developed the concept of "available" in her spiel, she slipped into what I at first thought were near-synonymous ideas. There is the notion of "being available," which suggests some choice on the part of the person. And there is the notion of "being made available," which shifts the agency to some higher power and blends with the idea of "chosen." That some distinction needed to be made instantly became obvious when I asked her to identify the point at which she knew she was chosen and available, whereupon she responded: "I am not chosen yet. I am available; I've always been available." During what became three pages of transcript, I harassed her about why she insisted on saying that she was not chosen, and wasn't this, in the final analysis, some semantic stubbornness. What, I wanted to know, would being chosen look like on her such that what I see is not already that? She replied that she did not really know: "I think the mission, the quest would be clearer, would be more manifest as a quest. I'm not so much on a quest, have never been on a quest, as I am just hanging around. I'm hanging around, you know, being available. That's how I live. That's what I trust also."

This, Toni says, is very different from "pursuing an idea, a sound, a quest, a being." For that, "you have to be clearly looking for that god, you're clearly summoning, you're invoking that spirit." She devised the example of someone picking up a harmonica, invoking the gods, and wishing to be a masterful player so that they can heal. Unless the gods are perverse, then they would choose that person and she or he would be on her or his mission. It seemed to me that she, Toni, could decide to see her writing, for instance, in this way. However, the problem is, as she put it, "I can't get to certain words like *decide* and *will* and *intent* and whatever." "Deciding," she maintained, has nothing to do with the adventure she is having, the nature and shape of which she discovers and contributes to as it moves along: "This soul is having an adventure in this woman, this body, and we're hanging out, and it's being fun." She dubbed herself an "enabler" who can identify others on a mission and "play a part in other people's moving into that chosen light." That, however, is not where she is. What she does she simply would like to call her work.

Toni never defined "available" or "chosen" in a mode that would suit a dictionary. However, she spoke enough about them in various ways to convey their meanings. Emanating from sources and reasons unknown (but sources and reasons that we would tend to think of as divine or universally powerful), being chosen is a definite kind of willed and focused receptivity that brings to a person what is necessary for the fulfillment of a fervently desired and beneficent or useful aim. Someone who is available receives the same energies and forces, but the element of will is not a causative factor and the directional focus may be less clear. A person who is chosen would of necessity be available, but someone who is available may not be chosen—although this seems potentially problematic since how one arrives at that available state remains unknown, such that being in it may, in fact, represent a condition of "chosenness."

In any case, as I understand this, those who are "available" and "chosen" are both in service to "the gods." What is being described is a state of willing participation in the positive evolution of the planet. It is akin to the words of a hymn often sung in black protestant churches: "Here am I, O Lord, send me." Whether or not we know ourselves to be chosen, we ourselves can choose to be available to spiritual impression. This choice is, as Toni used to say about her writing, "a legitimate way to participate in struggle." Seeing that this is the case is a radical contribution to our understanding of how to "do" one's work in the world, including political work. And, it is further significant that African American women, who have contributed so much concrete activism, embrace this revolutionary, spiritual point of view. Thus, the many ways that we align ourselves with spirit are to be appreciated as socially contributory and valuable.

One of these ways, which directly utilizes the route of the pineal gland, is meditation. Many of the women whose stories and thoughts comprise this book are regular meditators. Others achieve the same results in different, less formal ways. The array of possible means is extensive. I sit in meditation every morning; Dolores Kendrick waits quiet and alone in contemplative prayer; Namonyah Soipan watches candles burning at her ancestral altar; Michele Gibbs gazes with relaxed concentration at a virgin sheet of amate prior to beginning her painting; Alice Walker engages in the Buddhist practice of *tonglen,* which involves breathing *in* what *is not* desirable (suffering, anger, hatred, etc.) and breathing *out* what *is* desirable (joy, peace, love, etc.); Geraldine McIntosh focuses her mind-being in silent, one-pointed thought as she plots how best to reach people in an upcoming workshop.

Being available enabled Toni herself to bring spirituality into her political and cultural work with unparalleled aplomb. And who can calculate the salutary expansions of consciousness sparked by the inspired and inspiriting musicality of Miles Davis and Billie Holiday? The more available we are, the more human and cosmic mysteries are opened to us. And the more useful we become as agents in the world.

Michele Gibbs and Toni Cade Bambara have led us to an important lesson. They have shown that being politically conscious and active also encompasses knowing and using the "spiritual seed" nature of the self to connect with and channel from the world of spirit and, from that world, to bring into this one ideas and inspiration needed to impact human consciousness at the deepest levels and effect real change. This description sounds like the creative process of the writers discussed in chapter 4, and rightfully so, for the mechanism and the overall work are fundamentally the same. From our "God-given" political identities we find spirituality, which produces creativity, which can then be utilized in a higher political service. Michele is accurate when she speaks in terms of "creativity and birth."

With so much transforming work needing to be done at this critical, transitional time in every area of human endeavor, the many ways that individuals strive to do good and make needful change are absolutely essential, from traditional materialist interventions such as occur through institutionalized political processes, to sitting in meditation and intuiting how to flood this beleaguered Earth with light and love. African American women help us to validate and appreciate it all, particularly the greater role that spiritual consciousness is beginning to play as we enter the upcoming age.

Taking On the Spiritual Struggle

So, from the hard-won place where creative spirituality is becoming operative for political ends, how do African American women, in Geraldine McIntosh's words, "take on spiritual struggle"? Geraldine herself draws on these energies in her corporate work. Sonia Sanchez specifically focuses on how spiritual struggle is relevant to and for diasporic African people. Finally, Lucille Clifton illustrates availability through her conscious cooperation with ascended teachers in order to bring their spiritual messages to Earth.

Generally, Geraldine chooses to rely on her instinctive powers until a heightened use of spiritual energy is required. Constantly, while at her job, she automatically interacts with people from her spiritually connected heart and soul space. But, when she walks into a formal meeting where she has to function as the diversity resource for her vice president, then, at crucial moments, she focuses and "calls together" all of her energy so that she will know what she needs to say—for example, to the individual who is deviating from the human relations guidelines. Geraldine concludes: "I have stopped saying that I should handle spiritual energy one way versus another, because it is the doing that is important. Whatever it is I'm picking up to tell that person in the meeting, it goes straight to the heart of the matter. It goes right there and even if their egos or their whiteness make them say something, fuss, argue, whatever their inner action is, they get something out of what I have said so that they can shift, they can move."

Because it is dynamic in quality, spiritually focused energy brings about shifts and movement. In other words, it triggers change. This is the reason for inviting it into our everyday lives. Geraldine elaborates:

Geraldine: I'm saying that moving, shifting, growing, internal growth make a space in your life for you to be able to connect to the next thing that should move you. Moving in the world requires that you struggle, and when I say struggle, I mean that—at some point—you have to take some new information and try to relate it to some old feelings and a new vision. But you're always trying to relate, like a triangle, trying to relate three things and one of these things is different. I'm not talking about struggle like slave labor.

Akasha: I got it.

Geraldine: I'm talking about a kind of spiritual struggle. Once you make that connection, then you shift somewhere else in your life. When you get there, there's a fire for a while, and then either the vision changes or the external data changes, something. The only thing that doesn't change is the path.

Akasha: But one of those three poles gets shifted?

Geraldine: Yes. Something shifts and I guess if you're lucky or something, you can connect into it, work, take on the struggle. Lots of people don't take on a struggle.

Akasha: No, they don't.

Geraldine: But when you take on that struggle, it is in that struggle that you are enabled to move and shift and I think it is that shifting that is the development of one's spirituality, and how open you are, and what can come into you.

What Geraldine describes here is, to coin a phrase, the dialectic of availability, and what that process can look like for a human being. She also firmly states that such shifting and growth are what life is all about.

When Sonia Sanchez speaks about spirituality, she is acutely sensitive to its racially inflected relevance for black people. She wants to raise consciousness about matters that are rarely talked about—black men being raped in slavery, children being sold in crack houses for a fix, a country that sells sex even as it hypocritically hypes morality to discredit a heroic figure like Dr. Martin Luther King Jr. Using her intuitive, spiritual faculties, she is able to envision this buried history and these obscured travesties and place them before the world.

Sonia declares that individuals who are somehow available to spirit are given information for the purpose of passing it on:

> That's why I'm here. That's why this information is here. That's why these departed souls are here. They are saying, "We're here because we have chosen you to continue this information. We know because you have been us." Some of those people that I talked to, I've been them, they've been me before. They come back with the information and say, "Ah, there you are, Sonia. I've been waiting for you, you know. I've been waiting for you for fifty years, here you are, or forty years or thirty. Here you are."

I wondered out loud whether these souls carried any specific historical or racial lineage. Sonia replied that she did not know and had never thought about it, although she assumed that these souls who spoke to her were African.

I posed my question about race because racial ancestry has a different meaning when approached from a spiritual perspective. There might be an evolutionary reason for our being in the particular raced bodies that we inhabit. If this is true, then, in order to live fully in them, to do our job of "redeeming" them, we must assume all the struggles and privileges that flow therefrom, fully immersed. If we credit the idea of the evolving soul, a pattern of soul growth might require repeated incarnations into a specific race. Through a particular body, we could also possibly carry perceptible reminders of former racial incarnations with which we were strongly marked. I once read that souls incarnate 777 times before they complete their journey. In the course of that many lifetimes, one would perforce assume many racial identities. Therefore, the soul's point of view would transcend race. However, only in this spiritual sense is race meaningless, irrelevant, fallacious, insignificant, or defunct. On the physical plane, the bodies we are in profoundly matter.

At this point, we have come completely around the politics-spirituality-creativity circuit, looking at our most basic selves—who we are in our material bodies in a material world—from the angle of creative spirituality. Sonia's remarks about the significance of race draws on this wisdom, especially when she discusses the need to come to terms with racial identity. A portion of my interview with her reveals this:

> **Sonia:** We're living at a time when it is necessary for people to identify themselves as certain people just because they were identified as those people in the past in ways that disempowered them. So, at some point, people will have to get what I call a racial identity in order to

move on. If you never had it, then you end up doing all kinds of things, mutilating the self and mutilating other people because you really don't know who you are. When you do know who you are, then you're less prone to do that, and then you're more open to other kinds of things as well.

Akasha: Because you have a self that knows?

Sonia: And also you have a self that can finally divide. But if you don't ever have that self, it can't divide. I think what it does is to atrophy. It shrinks. Or it makes us look up and think that in order to be a human being, we must all be like white folks and imitate them and take on what they do. I think the worst thing this western world has done was to rob the African of her or his identity, and it did so because of control and power. And so what we're doing is wresting control, trying to empower ourselves. Once you empower yourself, you begin to understand how that can move out, how that can spread. And you also begin to understand that, more than likely, we have been empowered by a lot of people, a lot of forces within us. But the idea is to deal with the forces that identify us at any particular point.

Here Sonia declares the necessity for all people to come to terms with and rightly live in their particular racial identity. She says this is crucial if that identity has been eviscerated or otherwise weakened in the past. Not doing so can lead to what she terms "mutilation" of the self and of others. At this point, she shifts her focus to apply these understandings to black people.

One virulent form that our mutilation takes is to worship and imitate white people. If racial mastery is not cultivated, especially by people of color, misidentifications on both personality and spiritual levels by those in power can kill the emergent self. Hence the need for African-derived people to wrest control from negating white definitions and become empowered. And, in this work, ancestral spirits (defined in the largest, even aracial, spiritual sense) can play key, enabling roles. Ultimately and clearly, race is a necessary starting place. Once positively apprehended, it becomes a platform of strength from which wider identities can be embraced. This is what Sonia means when she speaks about having a self that can "divide."

Black people's spirituality—if acknowledged and consciously used—could be an awesome force. Even functioning as it has in a less-than-ideal manner under crippling circumstances, it has been a potent vehicle for good. In pointing this out, Sonia reminds all of us of the metaphysical role people from the African continent and the triangular slave trade have played in the spiritualization of the globe. Speaking of what she sees as the upcoming "wide, long battle," waged extensively "on a very spiritual level, where we're trying to move people," she declares: "As African people, we have moved people spiritually in this country. This country is sustained through the spirituality, I think, of African people." Via music, humor, how we walk or hit a ball, helping people to feel good about themselves so they are less prone to render hurt—Sonia says—"we are in a sense humanizing the world." However, as African American people, we must progress beyond these hip and humanizing externals into an even more effective spiritualized political consciousness:

Sonia: Yes, this is form, but there's something underneath it. These heavy arms, these legs, these feet—mostly water. And what does that mean? That if you pollute the body, then you'll pollute the ocean.

Akasha: And to know that they're one and the same. More and more people are getting that these days.

Sonia: Yes, but not enough. And certainly it's very difficult for people to understand that when their jobs depend on it. It's difficult to say to workers at nuclear plants, "We're going to shut down these plants," and they say, "Hey, I need a job." So, I'm saying that the whole world need, then, is not only to raise the consciousness, but also . . .

Akasha: Change the conditions, so that the consciousness can have a place to live.

Sonia: Exactly. So that's why I was talking to you about people who have a spiritual consciousness who are not activists, people who will have a shrine and an altar but will not get out there and effect change. I say that's wasted energy.

Such spiritual energy must not be wasted, but rather, it should be focused on conditions in the world that need redeeming.

Lucille Clifton dramatically demonstrates the life of blessing and service that can result when we make ourselves available, allying our concentrated strength with the spiritual energies of the universe. Acting thusly, she has been an inspirational force and a conduit for information from suprahuman realms. By the time she had accepted her psychic abilities and her communications with her dead mother, Lucille had similarly been in contact with other nonphysical beings. In 1975 and 1976, she received messages from The Ones Who Talk, who, when asked, said they did not have names. She was asked to come every morning to "receive a message for our world"; and despite the fact that she was a morning sleeper, she was faithful to this calling—even when she was traveling.

She rose every morning at 7 A.M. for seven months and yawningly transcribed communications about "the fate and danger of the world of the Americas" from The Ones Who Talk. They said they were interested in how America would proceed, and, as Lucille put it, their words were also interesting. They talked about avatarship and those who have come at former times as avatars, incarnated gods, embodied as people, who serve humanity as aids and models. However, their primary focus was "the perilous state in which the world was now." This particular time was called "the world of the Americas" because the United States has so much influence (whereas at other times, there had been other "worlds"). They said that if the country does not change its ways, then "the patience of the universe will wear out and the natural result of America's actions will be allowed to continue."

Lucille has encompassed some of what she was told by these Ones into an unpublished nineteen-poem sequence called, "the message from the ones." The poems are pithy bits of wisdom and advice. The beings first call themselves "ones / who have not rolled / selves into bone and flesh." They then rhetorically raise these questions: Why would they wish to do so? Why would they want to incarnate themselves?

why should we wander boneyards
draped in linen
flesh is the coat we unfasten
and throw off
what need to linger among stones
and monuments
we have risen away from all that
wrapped in understanding

The Ones Who Talk present an image of ghosts haunting grave-yards, still tangled in their linen shrouds, looking for human hosts and reluctant to leave the human world. They reject this popular scenario of horror stories, telling us of their happiness to fling off flesh, which they metaphorically refer to as a confining coat. Thus released, they attain a state of "understanding," far surpassing anything they had known on Earth, a state which serves as a far better set of clothes.

To try to further explain who they are and how they exist, they say to us: "we are here / between the lines / you reach through us / to raise your morning cup." They know, of course, that we who feel ourselves "drowning in the body's need" cannot really comprehend "fleshlessness," and therefore they attempt to make it even plainer:

there is no hunger here
we come to you directly
without touching
you who lie awake
holding your mouth open
receive us as best you can
and we enter you

as we must

tongueless

as best we can

As is apparent from these lines, their attempt to make their non-corporeal state clear to us pushes them into paradox. It is always difficult to put metaphysical matters into words. First, they come to us "directly," but this is nothing like physical "touch." Secondly, I believe that, when they speak about those human beings who lie awake holding their mouths open, they are alluding to individuals who are in various ways available to them. In those postures of readiness, we receive as much of what they impart as we can, which is difficult because The Ones Who Talk do not speak in language. They are, in their word, "tongueless." Later, to those who "have been blessed / or cursed / to see beyond yourselves" (the psychics and the otherwise spiritually attuned), they point out that everything has not been seen or said by us and that they have noticed what we either have not noticed or have ignored.

The Ones impart other information, too, about the spiritual world and about human contact with it. Angels have no wings, but wear "their own clothes" and, because they have learned to love us, will keep coming unless we "insist on wings." They say that, from the perspective of "life / blessed," being human is neither wiser nor more blessed. They repeat the ancient, fundamental lessons about love and karma, what they (or Lucille as poet) term "the same old / almanac": "january / love one another / february / whatever you sow / you will reap." Add to this, "you are not your brother's or sister's keeper, you are your brother or sister," as Lucille stated this last lesson, in her own person, "Life is kin. I believe that. I know it, in fact. Some things I believe, some things I know."

The final five poems in the series contain the warning messages, which are that we have placed ourselves and our world in peril by our focus on the insignificant; that "balance / or be balanced" is the law of the universe; that we will eventually have to breathe the air we pollute and drink the water we poison; and that the universe, grown impatient, might "slowly / turn its back" and "walk away." These are all injunctions that most of us have heard before. However, they repeat them because we have still not paid heed. The Ones Who Talk put their grave sentiments into a cosmic context when they tell us that:

> there are some languages
> some fields some sky
> the lord of language field and sky
> is lonely for
> they have been worlds
> they will be worlds again

Furthermore, on a star "more distant / than eden," something is "even now / preparing."

They are letting us know that our planet, our universe even, is not the only one there is, or has been, or will be. Thus, they seek to give us some perspective on our place in a very huge cosmic scheme, seemingly to apprise us of both our worth and our relative insignificance. If the finally out-of-patience "universe" "turns its back" and "walks away" from us, it will not be the end of the world. The "lords" can become at will languages, fields, skies, and worlds. Ancient wisdom teachings say that great beings who have achieved vast states of consciousness as planetary or even solar entities voluntarily diminish and retract themselves in order to oversee the development of particular aspects of creation and evolution. This is a process that replicates on a grander scale the sacrificial descent into incarnation that human souls are thought by some to make repeatedly.

Lucille has looked for opportunities to share her "message from The Ones," but, so far, for whatever reasons, it has not been published. She has also produced "several manuscripts" that utilize her experiences with the supernatural, including the miraculous happenings in her own family. Her agent, who, by the way, believes her experiences with the supernatural are genuine, suggested that she might want to write this material under a pseudonym. Lucille granted that this was a feasible idea—except she believed that the reputation she has earned under her own name would give the work credibility, since people would say, "This is kind of weird, but Lucille is generally not nuts like that." However, the publishers she approached were upset because, in her words, "nothing was like *The Amityville Horror.* That kind of Hollywood ghost stuff doesn't happen, that's not real." The publishers wanted something much more "sensationalistic." They further questioned her as to what she would do if somebody said they did not believe her. She replied, "I would understand that." Not "hung up" about any of it, her conclusive words on the subject are that "it doesn't matter."

And, true, it does not matter in the sense in which Lucille means it—that is, that her individual happiness or productivity is not dependent upon whether skeptical and profit-oriented establishments accept her spiritual reality. However, it greatly matters to us all that we collectively meet the challenge of learning how to apply to our current world situation the wisdom of group love and responsibility that The Ones Who Talk have presented through her. By heeding Lucille's message, and ourselves becoming channels for the higher, transpersonal energy that empowers us to take on struggle in a divinely inspired way, we close the transformational circle of creative, spiritual, and political power.

AFTERWORD

I did not participate in the revolutions of the 1960s as I would have wished; my family upbringing was more fearful than activist, and where I found myself at key moments was not particularly conducive to racial activism. In the late 60s, I felt isolated as a young, married, graduate student and mother at Purdue University in Indiana. I was programmed to succeed academically, holding on to a raced and racial identity, wearing an Afro and long African-print skirts, but without any community of support and without a sufficient history of consciousness to be self-starting and creative enough to figure out how to exist more fully in the movement.

Since then, one ongoing concern has been to make my academic work as activist as possible, which I have done by championing authors who were excluded from the canon of accepted literature; recovering and valuing neglected and underappreciated black women writers; taking radical black-feminist stances;

adopting a pedagogy that critiqued social injustice, brought politics into the classroom, and empowered the learners. I have even begun teaching a course, "Spirituality in African American Women's Literature," bringing into the university classroom knowledge and ways of knowing that are unorthodox. Still, I felt the nagging sensation that the impact I was making was not direct enough.

Not until I began, in 1991, the process that has become this book did I feel that I had found the one thing that was mine alone to do—a reason, perhaps, for being on this earth, a piece of work that everything in life had led up to, a task that required all of the best that could be given, a challenge that would try, test, heal, and transform. Ultimately, the writing of *Soul Talk* has been a spiritual journey. It has had a purpose larger than me, and has been guided and informed by that purpose. It has been the means through which I have come to know myself as a spiritual entity, part and parcel of a spiritual universe.

Before I could complete it, I had to begin recovering from sexual abuse and other psychic wounds and start to build an authentic identity. Until I struggled to become a whole and complete self on every level—physical, emotional, mental, and spiritual—I could not make a whole and unified book. This meant, for instance, revisiting the desire I had harbored as the editor of the Booker T. Washington High School *Lion's Roar* to become a journalist and feature writer. Heartbreakingly turned away from attempting this profession because of its risks and uncertainties for even a bright poor southern black girl in the early 1960s, I had poured this thwarted energy into books and articles that pushed the limits of academic writing but also provided formal shelters behind which I could disappear. To do the work of *Soul Talk,* I had to find my way back—or forward—to another kind of original voice and creative style.

From 1993 onward, my meditation, study, and daily spiritual practice had deepened. Contact with my own soul/spirit had been sparked. Once this occurred, the guidance for this work became stronger and more operative. Nevertheless, during this time, I could experience my not writing the book, not getting it done swiftly, only as a major problem. Beset by uncertainty and frustration, I procrastinated, floundered, conducted peripheral research, veered down unnecessary avenues, took wrong turns, concocted various outlines and proposals, wrote pages and chapters that in the end would not be used. Having concluded the project, I have enough outtakes to make another book.

I see now that the real preparation was not the uncertain research and writing of drafts. It was what my soul/spirit was teaching me as I studied and meditated. I was learning the wisdom handed down through the ages about the constitution and operation of the spiritual universe. I was gaining enough theoretical and experiential understanding about spirituality to write this book. I was being sorely tried, being taught faith, humility, and patience, as well as forging self-integration and true self-esteem. All that time, this was my real "research" and preparation, not the old tried-and-true spinning of scholarly wheels.

As I pursued my spiritual practice, the existence of the soul or higher self became a fact and a reality in my life and not only a belief and a hope. I saw it and felt it and experienced its beneficent effects. I learned beyond a shadow of a doubt that the spiritual universe is another, inner world, complete with its own inhabitants, occurrences, and laws; that angels and masters and continuously occurring events present themselves on astral and mental planes. And I realized that we could all be in conscious contact with this vast and amazing kingdom. Oriented as I had been toward a spirituality that was predominantly intellectual and "heady," I also had to fall to the knees of my heart. One day, as I was despairing about this book and my life in general, I heard a voice say to me, "Talk to God." Not pray, but talk to God. I didn't know how. And I realized that in my ultra-sophistication, I had never sought solace in that simple, human act, had never unburdened my heart into the all-accepting matrix of the universe.

Finally, I began to grasp the mechanism of creation and creativity, whether of a universe or a poem—how essential concepts exist in the universal mind or the "mind of God," how we are able to tune in and grasp them, how we pass them "down" through our clarified minds and desiring aspiration into actuality upon the physical plane. Without some sense of this, I would not have been able to fathom what the writers said to me about how they made their art. I would not have understood what was happening to me as I struggled to birth this book, my own divinely inspired creation.

In March of 1996, on what I would later realize was Toni Cade Bambara's birthday, I was in a motel room by the ocean in Cayucos, California, on a personal and writing retreat. Toni had died the preceding December. Here at Cayucos three months later, with the fire to which she was attracted burning in a red candle, I distinctly felt Toni's presence and a kind of blessing, and, for the first time, pulled together a scheme that seemed really right. It, in fact, proved not to be the final form, but this work moved me closer to it than I had ever been and rekindled my enthusiasm. At this same time, I was having increasing difficulty keeping my life together, going to my job, and taking care of the myriad responsibilities that defined me. I had begun therapy that February, on Valentine's Day, finally convinced that I needed more help than I alone (even with all of my self-help books) could provide.

As the spiritual undertow that powered the book waxed stronger and stronger, over the course of the year, my outer life and its structure eventually broke down. I took a medical leave of absence from work, sold my house in Santa Cruz, moved to a small ranch with my partner in the foothills of Salinas, and began, for the first time in my entire life, to "do nothing"—because that was all that I could do. Stopped dead in my tracks, I had to learn to *be,* and to *become.* I spent long, late-spring and summer days stretched out on the ground or propped under a liquid amber tree, gazing at brown hills covered with chaparral and oak, listening to the cascading rising and fall of the wind. Only then did the first viable concept for *Soul Talk* come to me.

In retrospect, it does not surprise me that the turning point occurred out in nature, on a sunny knoll of St. Augustine grass among the birds. I am reminded of Alice Walker in the Mendocino country sitting by her pond and talking to Shug and Harpo. I recall her saying to me that the reason I was so smitten with *The Color Purple* was that it represented her "shimmering rebonding with nature" in a years-long phase of her artistic life. For the first time in twenty years, she was back in nature, drawing sustenance from it like the African giant Antaeus who lost his might when he could not touch the Earth. As my spiritual rebuilding started, so did the building of this book in its right, "destined" form. As I began the labor of constructing myself, stripped naked, from the inside out, from soul to external self, so *Soul Talk* began to be constructed, from divine idea to physical manifestation. This is how spirit operates—how it uses us, how it works us, does its work, forces us to do ours in the world.

What I wish for is that those who read this book will grasp the paradigm of creative, spiritual, and political power so compellingly enacted by progressive African American women, and ask themselves three sets of relevant questions about their lives:

- What is my political identity, how do I fit in and function within the hierarchies and dynamics of power that define both the United States and global society? Am I conscious of this personal situation and its meaning and implications for others and for the larger whole? If I am conscious, does this consciousness show up in how I act and what I do?

- Do I have a spiritual consciousness and/or practice that enables me to connect in an ongoing, useful, and sustaining way with the divine, procreative energy or entity that powers the universe? Does that connection foster in me a desire and urge toward positive growth, betterment, and loving relationship with the whole of life?

- How can I tell that my spirituality is operating effectively in my life, what are its visible, manifested, creative results? Am I relating better, more beneficially, more authentically with others? In what actions, behaviors, artifacts, products can my spiritualized creativity/creative spirituality be seen? Am I doing what, and as much as, I can? Am I accomplishing my work in the world?

The answers we could give to these questions can transform the world.

REFERENCES

African American Women on Tour Web site www.aawot.com. November 21, 2000.

Allen, Jenny. "Oprah's World." *US Weekly,* June 12, 2000.

Anderson, Jeffrey M. "Kasi Lemmons on *Eve's Bayou*" (A November 3, 1997 interview). Combustible Celluloid Web site www.combustiblecelluloid.com. November 21, 2000.

Bailey, Alice A. (with Master Djwhal Khul). *A Treatise on White Magic.* New York: Lucis Publishing Company, 1934.

Bambara, Toni Cade. *The Salt Eaters.* New York: Random House, 1980.

Bambara, Toni Cade. "What It Is I Think I'm Doing Anyhow." In *The Writer on Her Work,* edited by Janet Sternburg. New York: Norton, 1980.

Cameron, Julia. *The Artist's Way: A Spiritual Path to Higher Creativity.* New York: Putnam, 1992.

Clifton, Lucille. *Good Woman: Poems and a Memoir, 1969–1980.* Brockport, NY: BOA Editions, Ltd., 1987.

Dash, Julie. *Daughters of the Dust: The Making of an African American Woman's Film*. New York: The New Press, 1992.

Davies, Paul. *The Mind of God: The Scientific Basis for a Rational World*. New York: Simon & Schuster, 1992.

Ferguson, Marilyn. *The Aquarian Conspiracy: Personal and Social Transformation in Our Time*. New York: Jeremy P. Tarcher, 1980.

Jones, Roger S. *Physics for the Rest of Us*. Chicago: Contemporary Books, 1992.

Kendrick, Dolores. *The Women of Plums: Poems in the Voices of Slave Women*. New York: William Morrow, 1989.

Mbiti, John S. *African Religions and Philosophy*. Garden City, NY: Anchor Books, 1970.

Morrison, Toni. *Beloved*. New York: Plume/Penguin, 1987.

Morrison, Toni. *Song of Solomon*. New York: Plume/Penguin, 1977.

Morrison, Toni. *Tar Baby*. New York: Alfred A. Knopf, 1981.

Naylor, Gloria and Toni Morrison. "A Conversation." *Southern Review* 21, no. 3 (1985): 567–93.

"Out There: From *Independence Day* to *The X-Files*, America Is Hooked on the Paranormal." *Newsweek*, July 8, 1996.

Somé, Malidoma Patrice. *Of Water and the Spirit: Ritual, Magic, and Initiation in the Life of an African Shaman*. New York: Penguin, 1994.

Strouse, Jean. "Toni Morrison's Black Magic." *Newsweek*, March 30, 1981.

Sweet Honey in the Rock. *Good News.* Flying Fish Records, 1981.

Teish, Luisah. *Jambalaya: The Natural Woman's Book of Personal Charms and Practical Rituals.* San Francisco: Harper & Row, 1985.

This Bridge Called My Back: Writings by Radical Women of Color, edited by Cherríe Moraga and Gloria Anzaldúa. Watertown, MA: Persephone Press, 1981.

Thomas, Evan. "Hillary's Other Side." *Newsweek,* July 1, 1996.

Walker, Alice. "Writing *The Color Purple.*" In *In Search of Our Mothers' Gardens.* San Diego: Harcourt Brace Jovanovich, 1983.

Winfrey, Oprah. Official Web site www.oprah.com. November, 2000.

Zajonc, Arthur. *Catching the Light: The Entwined History of Light and Mind.* New York: Oxford University Press, 1993.

About the Author

Akasha Gloria Hull, Ph.D., is a writer, teacher, lecturer, and consultant who has published many groundbreaking books and articles that discuss African American women—especially previously unrecognized authors—from a black, feminist perspective. Her previous works include *All the Women Are White, All the Blacks Are Men, But Some of Us Are Brave: Black Women's Studies* (with Patricia Bell Scott and Barbara Smith); *Give Us Each Day: The Diary of Alice Dunbar-Nelson; Color, Sex, and Poetry: Three Women Writers of the Harlem Renaissance;* and *Healing Heart: Poems 1973-87.* She has been the recipient of a number of prestigious fellowships and awards, including those from the National Endowment for the Humanities, the Rockefeller Foundation, the Mellon Foundation, the Ford Foundation, the American Association of University Women, and the National Humanities Center. Ms. Hull has taught literature and women's studies at a variety of institutions, most recently as a professor at the University of California, Santa Cruz, and has widely presented on women, literature, power, and spirituality at conferences and workshops. A native of Shreveport, Louisiana and mother of one grown son, she lives with her partner on a small ranch in the California foothills between Monterey and Salinas.